THE CHALLENGE
OF COMMUNIST EDUCATION:
A LOOK AT THE GERMAN
DEMOCRATIC REPUBLIC

by
MARGRETE SIEBERT KLEIN

EAST EUROPEAN MONOGRAPHS, BOULDER
DISTRIBUTED BY COLUMBIA UNIVERSITY PRESS
NEW YORK

1980

EAST EUROPEAN MONOGRAPHS, NO. LXX

LA
772
K545

*To the memory of
my Mother,
Martha Siebert Klein
whose joy in
the beautiful things of life
remains a continuing source
of inspiration*

TABLE OF CONTENTS

ILLUSTRATIONS

(ADN Photographs Supplied by the GDR Ministry of Education)

TABLES

FIGURES

ABBREVIATIONS

CDU	Christian Democratic Union
COMECON	Council for Mutual Economic Aid
EP	Extended Polytechnical Secondary School
FRG	Federal Republic of Germany (West Germany) (*Bundesrepublik Deutschland*)
GDR	German Democratic Republic (East Germany) (*Deutsche Demokratische Republik*)
GP	Ten-Year General Polytechnical Secondary School
KPD	Communist Party of Germany (*Kommunistische Partei Deutschlands*)
MMM	Fair of the Masters of Tomorrow (*Messe der Meister von Morgen*)
NATO	North Atlantic Treaty Organization
SAN	Student Work Norms
SED	Socialist Unity Party (*Sozialistische Einheitspartei Deutschlands*)
SMA	Soviet Military Administration
TAN	Employee Work Norms
UTP	The Day of Instruction in Socialist Production (*Unterrichtstag in der sozialistischen Produktion*)
VEB	State-owned Enterprise (*Volkseigener Betrieb*)

PREFACE

The two German states—the German Democratic Republic (GDR) and the Federal Republic of Germany (FRG)—exist today at the cutting edge of East-West confrontation in central Europe. In the years since the defeat of fascist Germany in the spring of 1945 and their subsequent formation on October 7 and May 23, 1949, respectively, the GDR and the FRG have evolved into leading representatives of the two distinct major world systems. The FRG, an important ally of the United States, continues to evolve into a growing position of Western leadership. As a result of years of interaction between the two countries, West Germany has become a known entity to Americans—it is an opened society with many of its institutions patterned on Western systems, and it is readily accessible.

In contrast, the other Germany, the GDR, remains relatively unknown to the vast majority of Americans. Until recently, it existed in a state of limbo behind the iron curtain. However, with the opening of diplomatic relations between the United States and the GDR in November, 1974, unprecedented avenues of contact have developed which include some limited opportunities for first-hand reporting on various aspects of life in the GDR.

In July, 1975, I began an extended period of residence in Berlin as the wife of an American diplomat assigned to our embassy in the GDR. The opportunity that presented itself was initiatory. Aided by knowledge of the German language and a strong interest in international affairs, I was interested in learning about the education of young people in a socialist society. Compulsory education in the socialist countries is similar in structure and content, and an examination of the highly-developed East German model could provide significant insight into the goals, methods, and contents of contemporary socialist compulsory education elsewhere in Eastern Europe.

At the time of my arrival in the GDR, cultural agreements with the United States were nonexistent. Thus, in order to undertake the investigative work in which I was interested, it was necessary to develop a professional entrée with East German officialdom. Two months after having presented my credentials and research proposal to authorities in the GDR Foreign Ministry, I was informed that permission for undertaking the work had been granted. At a meeting at the GDR Ministry of Education, the specific areas in which the government agreed to cooperate were outlined as follows:

1. All required textbooks and curricula materials would be provided.

2. Professional educators active in areas related to my work would be available to answer questions according to the procedure that access would be channeled through and approved by the Ministry of Education.

3. Official visits to schools would be permitted for the purpose of observing instruction and meeting with teachers, the number of such visits to be determined by the GDR Ministry of Education.

4. Permission would be granted for an official visit to a pedagogical university where teacher training for the compulsory schools takes place.

In assessing these areas of cooperation, it is necessary to acknowledge the closed nature of socialist society in the GDR which severely limits access to existing institutions and imposes certain restrictions on the availability of information. Thus, with regard to the visits referred to above, the director of the International Section of the GDR Ministry of Education informed me that they represent the first instance that an American had been granted official permission to visit an East German compulsory school or a pedagogical university; GDR officials considered my proposed work to be of sufficient importance to warrant granting access to both types of institutions. Later, I was permitted another "first" in the form of a visit to a polytechnical centrum affiliated with several compulsory schools in East Berlin.

Clearly, the opportunity that was made available for reporting on the education of young people in the GDR was unique. In spite of the limited data-base made available, it still appears to have been adequate for developing a valid description of compulsory education in the GDR, since the limitations officially imposed on my freedom of movement in the research environment were sufficiently offset by the uniformity of instruction which exists throughout the country as a result of the centrally-controlled nature of GDR education.

Of equal significance for the validity and importance of a pioneering work such as this is the fact that I was able to live in the GDR for an extended period of time. This allowed my access not only to school officials, but, also, to extensive numbers of GDR citizens with children in the compulsory school system. The additional factor that I spent over two years doing reasearch and living in the GDR and that I made several subsequent working visits further offsets the restricted amount of information with which I was officially provided. The initial impressions of a foreign culture, colored by the psycological effect known as culture shock were thus surmounted and the superficial impressions often gained by scholars during short-term visits were overcome.

The approach to the present work reflects my contention that an understanding of any aspect of a society must be based on knowledge of the cultural foundation of that society. In the case of the GDR, the socio-economic and political structure of this socialist society is sufficiently different from our own to warrant an examination of its philosophical-ideological basis. For example, the conscious inclusion of political ideology into courses of instruction in all academic areas in the GDR, including the sciences, is a phenomenon unfamiliar to most Americans. In order to understand the reasons for this practice and the manner in which it is accomplished, one must examine the Marxist-Leninist foundation of East German society. The first two chapters of this book—"GDR Education in Historical Perspective" and "Topics in Communist Ideology"—are intended to provide the essential background necessary for understanding the education of young people in the GDR in its social context.

Four major areas of significance for Western educators are contained in the present work. First of all, the educational system in the GDR is centrally directed and controlled at the national level, in contrast to the decentralized systems of education with which educators in the United States and the West are generally familiar. Pedagogical scientists in the GDR are compelled to implement the most effective educational program possible during the compulsory school years for the purpose of preparing GDR youth for productive lives in socialist society. In particular, it is perceived that they must be educated to make positive contributions to furthering the technological and economic development of their country in the year 2000 and beyond. It is, consequently, of vital importance and critically urgent for Western educators, reared in the traditions of democratic society, to know what Communist educators consider to be the optimum educational preparation for life in the coming technological age.

Secondly, the present work provides the opportunity for acquiring an understanding of the goals of socialist compulsory education as it has evolved in the GDR. An interesting point of consideration in this regard, and part of the larger question concerning the degree to which political and social conditions within a society affect the functioning of its schools, is the extent to which the socio-economic structure of GDR society influences the educational program and curricula used.

GDR educators take the position that modern developments in technology and the significance of these developments in the life of every individual indicate that the sciences as well as elements of technological culture, i.e., the theoretical study of technology, and the mastery of certain technical capabilities are an important aspect of contemporary general education. This is a third area in which this book is of valuable significance for Western education. The implementation of this position vis-à-vis science and technology in the GDR has resulted in the polytechnization of general education. As a consequence, the natural sciences and mathematics have attained a stronger and broader position and instruction in these subjects has become more closely linked to the requirements of a modern industrial society. An examination of the effect of a polytechnical emphasis on education is warranted under the circumstances of the relatively mature level of development of the concept that has been achieved in the GDR, especially since (1) technology has an enormous influence on contemporary life in industrialized societies and (2) the introduction of an element of technology into the general education of young people has received serious consideration in many schools outside of the socialist orbit where the significance of science and technology in the core curricula is generally understated.

Finally, competition in the area of education is an aspect of the overall competitive posture assumed by the socialist societies with respect to the traditional democratic nations of the West. This fact emphasizes the validity and importance of acquiring an understanding and knowledge of the education provided for young people in socialist countries such as the GDR. Effective utilization of this type of information in the field of education may ultimately contribute to the survival of Western democratic traditions; it is in this spirit that the present work is offered.

A survey of the literature available in this area reveals that published material dealing with compulsory education in the GDR and the related topic of polytechnical education and training falls predominantly into two categories: material written in the GDR, and material written in the FRG. There is a striking absence of literature on these topics outside of the German sphere.

Professional literature concerning the topics of compulsory general education and polytechnical education and training is published in the GDR only after being scrutinized for doctrinaire consistency. It is understandable that all of this material is written from the basic premise that the Marxist-Leninist interpretation of reality is unique in its validity. Although an abundance of literature exists in this category, English translations are virtually nonexistent. Works published in the FRG on the subject of GDR education are limited in quantity and frequently suffer from a political bias, since West German scholarship, in view of its proximity, often tends to view the GDR much more from a subjective rather than an objective position. Additionally, there are no English translations of literature in this category. Thus, it is apparent that an information gap exists that needs to be filled, not only in the area of the education of young people in the GDR, but as it concerns the social, economic, and political basis of contemporary socialist general education. *The Challenge of Communist Education: A Look at the German Democratic Republic* is a response to this need.

Acknowledgment is made of the cooperation of the government of the GDR in permitting such a pioneer study to be undertaken, as well as of the assistance rendered by officials of the GDR Ministry of Education. Although the information provided was limited and structured, the fact that the work was allowed to commence is noteworthy. Further acknowledgment is made of the assistance provided by pedagogical scientists of the Academy of Pedagogical Sciences of the GDR and the *Paedagogische Hochschule* "Karl Liebknecht" in Pottsdam, the director and science teachers of the 6th Ten-Year General Poly-Technical Secondary School in the Weissensee district of Berlin, and the director and instructors of the Polytechnical Centrum VEB Secura-Werke in Berlin. Additionally, I owe a debt of gratitude to Professor B. J. Chandler, former dean of the School of Education of Northwestern University, and to Dr. L. Carroll King, professor of Chemistry at Northwestern University, for their support and for their enthusiastic encouragement, which was an essential motivating factor underlying the present work; and, a note of thanks to Wolfgang Mendow for his kind and unfailing assistance. Most of all, my thanks go to my husband, Jacques, without whose sensitivity, patient understanding, and guidance this book would not have been possible; and to my children, Christian and Maia, who so graciously shared their mother with her work.

Bonn   Margrete Siebert Klein
April, 1979

INTRODUCTION

The German Democratic Republic was established on October 7, 1949 in the eastern part of Germany designated as the Soviet Zone of Occupation at the end of the Second World War. Article 1 of the constitution of the GDR states:

> The German Democratic Republic is a socialist state of German nation. It is the political organization of the working people in town and country-side who are jointly implementing socialism under the leadership of the working class and its Marxist-Leninist party.[1]

Thus, the GDR is a socialist society and, although other political parties are allowed to exist, the real political power belongs to the Marxist-Leninist Party, i.e., the Socialist Unity Party (SED). The GDR is a member of the Socialist bloc Council for Mutual Economic Aid (COMECON) and of the Warsaw Pact, with whose member nations it shares the common goal of development towards communism.[2]

The cultural and economic spheres of national life in the GDR are guided and controlled by the Central Committee of the SED according to the Marxist-Leninist principles of the Communist philosophical system. The controlling role of the SED makes possible the fusion of Marxist-Leninist ideology into virtually all aspects of GDR society and, consequently, Communist ideology pervades all areas of economic productivity, the sciences, and the educational system, as well as art, the theater, films, newspapers, periodicals, television, and radio. The resultant all-encompassing influence of Marxism-Leninism on life in the GDR is a phenomenon without corollary in the traditional democracies of the West.

The Communist conviction that Marxism-Leninism is inherently moral and correct serves as a basic reason for the lack of tolerance manifested towards other philosophical systems within socialist society. The party views itself as being in possession of a special, privileged knowledge, i.e., Marxist-Leninist philosophy, which includes: (1) what is considered to be the only correct interpretation of history and its ramifications; and (2) a unique tool, the dialectic, used to interpret present circumstances and plan future development. As such, it becomes a duty and, more than that, a moral obligation, for the party to share this knowledge with the rest of society, albeit on a simplified level for the purpose of facilitating comprehension. In the GDR, this effort at educating the general population towards a Marxist-Leninist world view is manifested in the infusion of Communist ideology into all aspects of life within the purview of the SED.

The most basic and concentrated efforts at educating and training the population of a socialist society towards comprehension and internalization of Marxist-Leninist philosophy are made during the mandatory period of education. In examining education in a socialist society such as the GDR, it is of utmost significance to realize that education is the essential means by which achievement of the ultimate ideal of a fully developed Communist society is expected, and that the basic education required of young people is fundamental to the realization of this goal. The curricula of the compulsory schools incorporate the basic values of Communist society and represent the current level of educational planning by Communist educators for the purpose of providing youth with the most comprehensive education possible so that as adults they may make an effective contribution to the further economic development of Communist society in the technological age.

Marxist-Leninist philosophy is the foundation upon which the educational system in a socialist society is developed, and education is an aspect of socialist society that is integrated into a comprehensive plan for producing economic results deemed beneficial for the further development of Communism. The visibility of socialist society— a fundamental indicator is its level of economic performance—is ultimately seen to be closely linked to the results of its educational effort. The rationale for this relationship is to be found in the dependence of a country's economic productivity on the level of development of its scientific and technological expertise. This factor, in turn, is directly related to the quality of scientific and technological training available in that society.

In the case of the GDR, an assessment of educational effectiveness on the basis of economic performance lends weight to the pride with which GDR citizens view their schools. The economic "miracle" that the GDR has succeeded in bringing about refers to the development of its national economy from devastation immediately after World War II to its present position as one of the world's ten leading industrial nations.[3]

The rise of the GDR to a relatively high-level economic status occurred despite the fact that it was paying heavy war reparations to the Soviet Union until 1954. The economy of the GDR continues to be integrated with those of the other Warsaw Pact nations with the result that a certain percent of the GDR's current economic productivity is siphoned for the economic benefit of the other socialist countries, in general, and for that of the Soviet Union, in particular, rather than for its own internal development. Despite this continued indirect economic exploitation, the GDR has achieved the highest level of economic performance of a socialist nation with the exception of the Soviet Union and, today, has achieved the highest standard of living in Eastern Europe.

The successful economic development of the GDR is considered to be important for the further development of communism for two reasons. First, since an increased level of national economic development is internally reflected in an elevated standard of living, a high rate of economic productivity is considered to be an important factor in consolidating the support of the population of the GDR for a communistic form of government. And, second, a high rate of national economic productivity is viewed as resulting in enhanced international status for the socialist government of of GDR and for the world Communist movement, in general.[4] Thus, it is assumed that economic success will legitimize the socialist government of the GDR at home as well as abroad.

The essential motivating factor for all economic activity in the GDR is the premise that direct relationships exist between (1) the rate of national economic development, (2) the degree of internal support for communism, and (3) the extent of international respect for the GDR. The basic purpose of all planning and activity in the sectors of national life which are controlled and directed by the Central Committee of the SED is to support the further development of the GDR national economy within the framework of the contemporary status of Marxist-Leninist theory. In the area of education, for example, the integral relation that exists between national economic development and compulsory education is accorded legal status in Article 69 of the Law on the Integrated Socialist Educational System of February 25, 1965, which states that:

(1) the Council of Ministers is responsible for the complex and coordinated planning and administration of the integrated socialist educational system.

(2) on the basis of the long-term and annual economic plans the Council of Ministers ensures the continuous further development and improvement of the socialist educational system in keeping with the requirements of social development, above all of the technolgocial revolution.[5]

The development of education in the GDR has been intimately related to the political and social changes that have led to the transformation of the GDR from a devastated portion of the former German Reich to a leading representative of contemporary socialist society. In order to acquire an understanding of the education of young people in the GDR in a social context, some insight into the historical development of East German education is essential.

CHAPTER I

GDR EDUCATION IN HISTORICAL PERSPECTIVE

The present system of education in the GDR has its origin in the defeat of Nazi Germany in the spring of 1945. Initially, the major factor motivating educational change was the tension that existed as a result of the ideological differences between the Communist orientation of the Soviet Military Occupation and a demoralized people conditioned by national socialism, as German fascism was called. The political scientist, George H. Sabine, described these differences in his book, *A History of Political Theory*: [1]

> Many of the similarities between national socialism and communism lie upon the surface and are manifest. . . . Despite these manifest similarities, however, it is certain that communism was on a far higher level, both morally and intellectually, than national socialism. . . . National socialism was at bottom political cynicism: the willingness endlessly to manipulate human nature by emotional intoxication and hysteria, not to realize a value but to aggrandize a self-styled elite which in truth was a gang. Communism was fanatical; but on the whole it was honest and at least initially its underlying purpose was generous and humane. . . . It had been born of a conviction which came to be shared by democracy, that the first impact of industrial technology and capitalism was dehumanizing and socially demoralizing, and its ultimate aims had been those of democracy itself.

Further:

> The political philosophy of communism formed, on the whole, a coherent and carefully developed body of thought. Lenin and Trotsky were indeed fanatics but they were men of convictions, standing in a long tradition of Marxian scholarship and party policy. Moreover, the achievements of communism in Russia were generally constructive. Despite the fearful price exacted by the brutality of Stalin, his rule transformed that country into a modern industrial power, and an illiterate peasantry into an educated people with a high level of science. No similar judgment can be passed upon fascism in Italy or national socialism in Germany. Their parties were mushroom growths from the demoralization of World War I; their leaders were demagogues; and judged by any standard of achievement, their careers were purely destructive. Their so-called philosophies were mosaics of ancient prejudices, put together without regard for truth or consistency, to appeal not to common purposes but to common fears and hates.

[5]

The task that confronted education was considerable. Essentially it involved the rehabilitation of a population that had come to accept, through active participation or acquiescence, the depravity of the human condition as a norm of existence.

Three factors of the immediate post-war period in Germany that have had a significant influence on the direction of the development of East German education are: (1) the general state of German education in May, 1945; (2) the ideological condition of the German population as a whole; and (3) the occupation of the East Zone of Germany by the military forces of the Soviet Union.

The educational system that had developed in pre-war Germany was elitist in the sense that it provided unequal educational opportunities. The greatest opportunities for intellectual development were reserved for the children of the upper-middle and upper socio-economic classes, while similar aspirations on the part of the children of workers and farmers were not encouraged. This elitism in education was a reflection of the rigid class structure that served as the basis of German society. It found its clearest expression in the tripartite educational system that developed.

Simply stated, the pre-war German educational system consisted of three parts: one which led to the possibility of achievement in higher education, a second led to white-collar employment opportunities at the mid-level of petty bureaucrats and trained technicians, and the third part prepared young people for vocations at the level of skilled and unskilled workers.

Before the unification of Germany under the leadership of Bismarck in 1870, the political decentralization of Germany provided conditions prerequisite for the growth of German cities into cultural centers. This development was the result of competitive efforts on the part of the ruling elites to imitate intellectual developments in other parts of Europe. As a consequence, universities and theaters flourished in towns such as Heidelberg and Goettingen, as well as in the large cities of Berlin, Leipzig, and Munich.[2] Another consequence, however, was that the control of education became decentralized by tradition and, in essence, the direction of school policy and planning remained the purview of the regional or state governments through the period of the Weimar Republic.

Although the decentralization of education resulted in the lack of standardization of school structures and curricula, certain generalizations can be made. Thus, the great majority of children attended the free elementary school, or *Volksschule*; the children of the lower-middle class attended the fee-paying intermediate school, or *Mittel-*

schule; and the secondary school, or *Hoehere Schule*, where the fees were twice those of the intermedidate school, were attended by the children of the upper-middle class. The rigid social structure and class awareness of German society as reflected in the school system were shown by the relative low frequency of transfer between schools and by the small representation in universities (6 percent in 1930) of youth from the class of skilled and unskilled workers, shop assistants, et cetera. i.e., from the lower classes.[3]

In March, 1933, Adolf Hitler assumed power and ushered in the terror of the Nazi regime in Germany, and little time was lost in forcing the educational system into a mold that conformed to the Nazi *Weltanschauung*. These efforts were aided by the enactment of a civil service law issued for the purpose of restoring the professional civil service which included teachers at the elementary school level.[4] The law enabled the Nazis to place reliable party members in crucial positions of the government bureaucracy, an important aspect of which was educational administration. Thus, national socialism found widespread support at all levels of the teaching profession as well as among the students. The most drastic efforts at nazification occurred in the educational methods and goals in the primary and secondary schools. Under the Nazi regime, education in Germany "became highly centralized, anti-intellectual, subservient to war preparations, and more vocational than ever"; and, "the numbers of university students were drastically reduced from 118,556 in 1931 to 49,543 in 1939. Only those whose racial descent, physical fitness, and record of service in the Hitler Youth were regarded as satisfactory were admitted to universities."[5]

A second factor influencing the origin of East German education in the immediate post-war period was the ideological situation. The German fascists had succeeded in deeply influencing a large part of the population ideologically, and, consequently, the most complicated aspect of the German educational situation of 1945 was the continuing influence of Nazi ideology among the teachers and the majority of children.[6] As a result of the extent to which the fascist indoctrination had permeated the thinking of the German nation as a whole, and in order to prevent its popular rebirth at some later time, the destruction of German fascism and militarism was a major objective of the Allied military governments in post-war Germany. This aim was enunciated under points 6 and 7 of the Potsdam Agreement:[7]

6. All members of the Nazi party who have been more than nominal participants in its activities to be removed from public and semi-public

office and from positions of responsibility in important private under-
takings. Such persons shall be replaced by persons who, by their political and moral qualities, are deemed capable of assisting in genuine democratic institutions in Germany.

and:

7. German education shall be so controlled as to eliminate Nazi and
militarist doctrines and to make possible the successful development of
democratic ideas.

The post-war ideological situation also contained elements of para-
doxical bitterness among the German masses. Bitterness towards the
fallen Nazi government was mixed with hostility, resentment, and re-
signation towards the Allied victors. Various groups with diverse
philosophical positions began articulating current values: among them
were Communists and Social Democrats who had survived Nazi per-
secution, and the Christian Democratic Union (CDU) which was
formed in part by members of the old Center Party and enunciated
the views of middle-class Protestants and Catholics. "The nationalistic
right and the more than routinely compromised members of the Nazi
Party disappeared, at least temporarily, from public life."[8]

The most significant factor influencing the origin of the East German school system was the Soviet occupation of the Eastern Zone
and the unique set of circumstances that this provided. In each of
the four zones of occupation, the occupying powers attempted to
reform the educational system, as well as other aspects of national
life, according to their own national ideals. In the western zones of
occupation these initial efforts at reform of the German educational
system were eventually thwarted by those Germans, "a clear majority, who, while they accepted the desirability of sweeping away Nazi
innovations, were inclined to regard the approach to education en-
shrined in pre-1933 institutions as essentially sound."[9]

In the Soviet Zone of Occupation, however, the *modus operandi*
for reform was differently conceived. First, the Soviet military command in the East Zone represented the social, economic, and political
system as it existed in the Soviet Union—an authoritarian, centrally-
directed government. Second, the stance of the Soviet Union vis-à-
vis the population in their zone of occupation was more that of the
victor to the vanquished than was the case in the British, French, and
American zones. The Soviet Union had paid a much greater price,
by far, for its victory. In the Soviet Zone there was little room for
lack of cooperation on the part of the German population: the Soviet
Military Administration (SMA) issued orders and the Germans in
their zone of influence had little alternative but to follow them.

These factors, then—the educational structure as it existed in May, 1945, the ideological situation, rife with hostility and requiring values capable of rallying the German population, and, the fact of the Soviet occupation—were the major elements that influenced the origin of the educational system in the GDR in 1945. From the point of view of the Soviet Union, the situation in Germany was one that begged reform and, as a consequence of their philosophical-ideological orientation, and perforce of their posture as victors over the German people in their zone of occupation, they had the power to do so.

At the onset of the Soviet occupation, the Germany that presented itself was ravaged and chaotic. In the words of returning émigrés:[10]

> The scene was like a picture of hell—flaming ruins and starving people shambling about in tattered clothing; dazed German soldiers who seemed to have lost all idea of what was going on; Red Army soldiers singing exultantly and often drunk; groups of women clearing the streets under the supervision of Red Army soldiers;; long queues standing patiently waiting to get a bucketful of water from the pumps; and all of them terribly tired, hungry, tense and demoralized.

And:

> We discovered a totally agonized people .... They were incapacitated by the poison of despair, a mixture of shellshock from the nights of bombing and war, of deeply ingrained fear of Bolshevism and the gradual awareness of their own guilt at everything that had befallen Germany.

Although a natural outcome of the disorder and difficult conditions, the extent of the brutal disregard for human values demonstrated by great numbers of young people was a legacy of their Nazi-influenced upbringing and of a pervading ignorance generally attributable to the low standards that characterized education in fascist Germany. The demoralization of young people

> grew to be a real danger. The streets, the ruins of the cities, and the "black markets" were the meeting places of children on the loose. Other school-age children belonged to gangs who stole and committed robbery with violence and other young people engaged in smuggling and prostitution.[11]

Many school buildings had been partially or totally destroyed. This was especially true in the cities and areas where there had been heavy bombing and extensive fighting over a long period of time. In the Soviet Zone, for example, the city of Leipzig had only twenty undamaged school buildings in 1945 as compared with 105 at the beginning of the war. In the Frankfurt-an-der-Oder region, 95 percent of the schools were either destroyed or damaged. In general, school buildings that were still usable often served as military hospitals, emergency housing, barracks, warehouses, or refugee quarters. Much of the furniture and teaching equipment disappeared in the last months of fighting and, in the spring of 1945, only 3,458, or 50 percent, of the 6,875 school building that were left undamaged in the Soviet Zone, excluding Mecklenburg, retained a full inventory. In Mecklenburg, itself, 39 percent of the schools had been either totally or partially destroyed.[12]

In addition to the fact that there were fewer schools, there were, at the same time, more children to fill them. Millions of refugees entered the Soviet Zone from the former eastern German territories and swelled the numbers of children and young people who were obligated to attend school to almost 500,000 more than in 1939. Against this bleak background and in view of the considerable difficulties, the resumption of classes in 10,822 schools in the eastern part of Germany on October 1, 1945 was, indeed, a remarkable achievement.[13]

The groundwork for this event was initiated on July 27, 1945 when the Soviet Military Administration issued Order Number 17 for the purpose of, among other things, restoring order to the educational system in the Soviet Zone. The German Central Administration for Education (GCAE), established as a result of this order, became the means by which changes in the organization of education in the Eastern Zone of Germany were to be effected. The tasks of the GCAE were to coordinate, guide, and control activities of school administrators throughout the Soviet Zone as well as to issue directives for the implementation of SMA orders regarding the transformation of German education.[14] In essence, Order Number 17 placed the power to mold the development of the East German school system in the hands of the Soviet Military Command and their agents in the GCAE. Thus, the GCAE was the agency through which the model of the Soviet educational ideal was to be made practicable at the working level in the Soviet Zone.

The goals and contents of education as they emerged in the Soviet Zone were not the creation of conditions in the immediate post-war months alone. The German Communist Party, the KPD, had begun to deal with the question of re-shaping the school system in the East Zone of Germany in the Soviet Union as early as 1944 when the Politbureau of the KPD set up a twenty-member commission to determine:

> how the entire curriculum would have to be changed in order to free the youth of all fascist and other imperialist influences. In addition, the draft documents contained numerous ideas for the shaping of a democratic school system that would completely abolish the educational privilege of the big bourgeoisie even though the system was as yet not of a socialist character.[15]

Reconstruction of East German education was based on this kind of prior planning and motivated by the agreement signed in Potsdam in May, 1945, as well as by a joint appeal of the central committees of the KPD and the Socialist Party of Germany (SPD) calling for a democratic reform of the schools. General goals were to make education uniformly available to all children and to put the school in "close and permanent interrelation with the economic, ideological, and political life of the people."[16]

The restructuring of East German education received legal sanction on June 12, 1946, with the publication and promulgation of the Law on the Democratization of the German Schools.[17] This law established (1) that all children were to have equal rights to education in accordance with their abilities and interests and regardless of property, religion, or origin; (2) that education is the responsibility of the state and private schools are forbidden; and (3) that the former system of primary and secondary schools was to be replaced by a unitary common school for the period of compulsory education. Thus, a uniform, compulsory, basic eight-year school and a centralized educational system were established, and two major features of pre-war German education were eliminated in the Soviet Zone—the decentralized nature of education and the tradition of educational elitism. The main provisions of the Law on the Democratization of the German Schools were subsequently incorporated into the constitution of the German Democratic Republic when it was founded on October 7, 1949.

The first uniform curricula for use in the schools were published during the summer of 1946:

> The new curricula clearly outlined what was to be taught in each subject to realize the antifascist democratic aims of education. . . . According to the curricula of July 1, 1946, all pupils in the upper classes of the basic schools received scientifically based training in mathematics, physics, chemistry, biology, German and so on, as well as in one foreign language. Instruction in these subjects had been confined to a small percentage of pupils in the lower classes of the grammar school up to 1945. . . .[18]

However, as the *Taeglische Rundschau*, the SMA daily newspaper, noted, "one could write excellent textbooks, work out great syllabuses and find progressive methods of instruction, but it would be a waste of time if there were no teachers capable of putting them into practice."[19] The Soviet military administrators and their indigenous agents realized that the locus of educational development would be easily influenced by the ideological orientation of the majority of teachers and that the future control of the educational system would, to a great extent, be determined by the ideological posture of the teaching body in the immediate post-war years.

Teachers were in serious short supply in the Soviet Zone at the end of the war. Many of the younger teachers had been called to active duty before the end of the war and, of these, many had been killed or taken prisoner. Another reason for the teacher shortage was that many teachers were found to be ideologically unfit for further teaching assignments. As noted earlier, teachers in Germany were also civil servants and, as such, were required to sign an oath of allegiance to the German state. At any given time, therefore, German teachers were generally defenders of the status quo. It has, in fact, been suggested that the teachers in Germany were a major force in influencing and preparing the mentality of the masses for receptiveness to Nazi ideology. In any case, the Nazis found widespread support at all levels of the teaching profession when they seized power.[20]

In the summer of 1945, the remnants of the German teaching profession were of questionable ideological persuasion. Of the 39,348 teachers in the Soviet Zone, for example, 28,179, or 71 percent, had been members of the Nazi Party; 20,000 were dismissed from further service in the schools after careful screening. Thus, on January 1, 1946, only 8,037 teachers who had been "simple" Nazi Party members remained in Germany's Eastern Zone and some of these were also dismissed in the following months.[21]

The sudden loss of over 20,000 teachers—more than 50 percent of the teaching body at the end of the war—resulted in a critical situation for the schools. In order to alleviate this shortage and help fill the 60,000 needed teaching positions, a cadre of *Neulehrer*, or "new teachers," were recruited primarily from the ranks of the working class and included "young workers, peasants, clerks, office employees, and other working people."[22] The major qualification they had in common was a willingness to work with young people in order to purge them of the taint of fascism.

Neulehrer were trained in eight-month courses that were initiated on instruction of the SMA in all *Laender* and provinces at the beginning of 1946. Fifteen thousand of these new teachers began teaching during the 1945-46 school year and another 25,000 in the 1946-47 school year. By the fall of 1946, two-thirds of all teachers in the Soviet Zone were *Neulehrer*.[23] Although they worked under unfavorable conditions imposed by scanty training, inadequate facilities, and feelings of animosity on the part of many students and parents with lingering fascist notions, the persistence and dedication of the *Neulehrer* alleviated the critical teacher shortage in the post-war years.

During this post-war period, developments in the political area included the formation in April, 1946, of the Socialist Unity Party (SED) through the union of the KPD and the SPD. By 1948, after a period of consolidation, the SED dominated political life in the Soviet Zone. The priorities and contents of school policy began to change from building a democratic, integrated school to strengthening the ideological and political work of the teachers. Efforts were also made to improve teaching standards, since qualified personnel were needed to help build up production capabilities to meet requirements for the economic reconstruction of the East Zone formulated at the SED's First Party Congress in January, 1949.

Although two separate German states were already envisioned in 1948—a constitutional convention met in Bonn on September 1, 1948, to draft a basic law for the formation of a separate West German state and the following November the People's Council in the Soviet Zone began drafting an East German constitution—efforts at seeking a German reunification continued, especially on the part of the Soviets, until the newly elected president of the FRG took office in September, 1949. The Soviets responded on October 7, 1949 with the founding of the German Democratic Republic, and transfered SMA functions to the provisional government. Educational reforms that had been made in the East Zone to date were written into the constitution of the GDR, in articles 34 through 40.

Although the GDR had been constituted as a separate entity, its existence remained precarious until the middle of 1952, because the Western powers as well as the Soviet Union continued to be interested in the possibility of German reunification. Indeed, the rationale of the West in creating the FRG was that a vital and strong West Germany would eventually lead to reunification of the two German states. On the other side, the Soviet Union urged support for German unity and withdrawal of all military forces from within the German boundaries. In between was the SED which was obliged to support the Soviet position, but which, at the same time, quite naturally was interested in maintaining its own role.

The reunified Germany that each side had in its mind's eye was one that was economically viable, military impotent, and politically acceptable. The obstacle, of course, was presented by the last. Efforts at reaching an agreement, nevertheless, continued with the major initiative, again, taken by the Soviet Union which sought quadripartite discussions. The West, however, opted against joining in the Soviet efforts and on May 26, 1952, the United States, Great Britain, and France together with the FRG signed the contractual agreements which gave West Germany internal independence and paved the way for its rearmament. This move effectively ended the question of German reunification. Soviet policy shifted to one of support for the GDR and the first deliberate steps were taken to convert the GDR into a socialist state.[24]

These events played themselves out against the background of the cold war. As a result of the Communist coup d'état in Czechoslovakia on February 25, 1948, a growing anti-communism in the West led to the creation of NATO and, subsequently, the inclusion in it of the FRG. From the GDR's perspective, the founding of the FRG and the creation of NATO, as well as the West's pervasive cold war mentality, were seen as continued threats to its survival.

The GDR's precarious existence at this time encouraged a rebellious attitude on the part of many East Germans, an attitude fueled by their previous anti-Communist conditioning as well as by their desire for German reunification. In an effort at stabilizing the ideological situation, the SED ordered instruction in all schools to be based on a Marxist-Leninist orientation. Accordingly, in September, 1951, new textbooks and curricula were introduced which based compulsory education in the GDR on the world view of Marxism-Leninism. Further aspects of the curriculum revision in the eight-year basic school was an expansion of the science program and some limited directives concerning polytechnical education.

In his welcoming address to the delegates of the Second Party Congress on July 10, 1952, Walter Ulbricht, then leader of the SED, called for the systematic construction of socialism in the GDR. The socialist reshaping of the schools was initiated a few days later. On July 29, the Political Bureau of the SED issued a decision which contained guidelines for school policy during the period of construction of the foundations of East German socialism.[25]

Ideological tensions that existed within the East German population in general were also reflected in the teaching profession. The source of these tensions was the fact that socialism in the GDR was not the result of an internal philosophical movement, but, rather, a revolutionary change imposed from above by the leadership of the SED and one that could not have been sustained without the presence of the Soviet military establishment.

Other contemporary socialist countries in Eastern Europe had similar origins. However, an additional complicating factor in the case of the GDR was the fact that there was the other Germany with which East Germans could identify, if not in fact then at least in wishful thinking. The emotional force of a common heritage of history, culture, and language, taken together with Western propaganda efforts aimed at subverting socialism in the GDR, played a fundamental role in undermining SED efforts at developing an atmosphere receptive to socialism in the GDR. The intensity of the Western effort in this regard is described in the following passage:

> The extent of Western pressure on the GDR is often underestimated. The economic drain caused by the continuing refugee drain is obvious. Equally apparent is the psychological pressure which an open border presented: the regime could not relax, neither could the population. What is less obvious, however, is the extent to which Western propaganda exacerbated difficulties in the East. RIAS—the U.S. Information Agency's transmitter in West Berlin—aimed a steady flow of disruptive propaganda at the Soviet Zone. The West German government did likewise.[26]

Major efforts at countering these pressures were made by the SED in the area of education. It remained to develop the schools into institutions where young people could be effectively educated and trained to become productive members of socialist society in the GDR. By 1952, some important steps in the development of the socialist school had already been implemented. These, primarily, included an educational program based on Marxism-Leninism, an overall Marxist-Leninist concept of the contents of general education, initial efforts at integrating vocational training with economic objectives, rejection of bourgeois educational views in favor of the Soviet experience, and a start at coordinating activities of the Communist youth organization with the work of the schools.[27]

German translations of Soviet pedagogical literature began to appear in the GDR in 1951. As the influx of these materials increased, the Soviet educational experience came to play an increasingly important role in the development of the East German socialist school. The traditional Marxist concept of polytechnical education had been revived by Stalin in the Soviet Union in 1952, but with his death in 1953 more urgent problems came to the fore, and polytechnical education remained a dormant educational issue until Krushchev called for its implementation in 1956.

.The polytechnical approach to learning is, today, the most remarkable feature of socialist education. The consolidation of the socialist school in the GDR is directly related to the evolution of the role of polytechnical education in instruction, and East German pedagogical science has had a major influence on its development. As already noted, early directives for introducing polytechnical education in GDR schools were contained in the curricula implemented in 1951. Within the context of these curricula, however, polytechnical education was intended as a method of science and mathematics instruction in the sense that technical applications were referred to in the instructional process.

Circumstances had a disruptive effect on the development of polytechnical education and, consequently, the Marxian concept of relating instruction and productive work was hardly regarded until 1956. In addition to the events that came in the wake of Stalin's death, another reason for this inactivity in the GDR is to be found in the results of a conference convened in Berlin in 1953 for the purpose of finding a means of implementing polytechnical education in the East German schools. The general conclusion of those attending a conference—including teachers and pedagogical scientists as well as representatives from industry, agriculture, and social organizations—was that the linking of instruction and productive work in a program for compulsory education was possible only in a future, developed Communist society.[28]

A further disruptive influence on the development of the socialist school in the GDR occurred during the late spring and early summer of 1956 when party and non-party intellectuals, motivated by the examples of Hungary and Poland, began acting on their own interpretations of Marxist-Leninist theory. Although these revisionist activities touched off discussions on every aspect of life in the GDR, they had no far-reaching effect on the population *per se*.[29] They did, however, have a disquieting effect on the body of teachers and, when the 5th Pedagogical Congress met in May, 1956, the SED's demands for progress towards the development of the socialist school were opposed by leading school functionaries.[30] The SED responded by organizing critical discussions of the revisionist views and initiating school experiments in polytechnical education in an attempt to close the gap between its leadership and the teaching profession.

A primary motivation for developing and implementing polytechnical education was the formulation of the concept in the socialist countries of a "scientific-technological revolution." This concept was introduced in the mid-1950's in an attempt to accelerate the economic development of these countries as well as their movement towards communism. Embodied in the political-ideological concept of a scientific-technical revolution was the hope that through the development of science and technology an economic state could be attained in the short term in which "strenuous physical labor would no longer be necessary, the differences between physical and mental labor would be reduced, and the satisfaction of all socially relevant

needs would be guaranteed."[31] Promotion of the scientific-technological revolution became a cornerstone of SED policy and it implied a
commitment in the GDR to the growing importance of science as
well as an expectation that worker qualifications would, of necessity,
become higher.[32] This meant that the compulsory schools were responsible for ensuring that young people would acquire a broad
scientific and science-related background on which they could later
build vocations that would contribute to East German economic
development. Thus, there were two basic factors that motivated the
SED to implement polytechnical education: polytechnical education
had both an economic and a social relevance.

Between 1956 and 1958, a variety of investigations concerning the
implementation of polytechnical education were made at individual
schools. The fundamental problem was that of finding an effective way
of combining instruction and productive work and of applying the polytechnical concept in all instructional areas for developing a Marxist-
Leninist world view in young people. During April 24-25, 1958, the
SED convened a school conference for the purpose of making the
following demands vis-à-vis the development of the socialist school:

> Accomplishment of polytechnical education and training with the
> goal that all students must have developed within them a socialist con-
> sciousness as well as a high regard for work and the working class. To
> that end it is necessary to educate the students in the foundations of
> production in socialist industry and agriculture, the most important as-
> pects of its technology, organization, and economics, and in practical
> work skills, so that they are able to work with measuring instruments,
> simple tools, and machines. That end is served by the introduction of
> an instruction day, in which the students from classes 7 through 12 to-
> gether with their teachers can learn and be productively active in the
> socialist operations of industry and agriculture... the transition from
> an 8-class elementary school education to a 10-class intermediate school
> education is foreseen for all children for 1965.[33]

Accordingly, on September 1, 1958, polytechnical education was
introduced in all compulsory schools throughout the GDR.

On December 2, 1959, the People's Chamber, or *Volkskammer*,
of the GDR adopted the "Law on the Socialist Development of the
School System in the GDR." It replaced all previous school acts and
ordinances and stipulated that: (1) the general school for all children
is the ten-year polytechnical school; (2) education and training are
to be closely bound up with productive work and with the activities
in socialist construction; (3) polytechnical education is a basic feature and an integral part of instruction and education in all school
classes; (4) the ten-year school is divided into a lower level comprised

of grades 1 through 4 and an upper level including grades 5 through 10; (5) the ten-year school furnishes the basis for vocational training; (6) after termination of the ten-year period of education, possibilities exist for further education; (7) the twelve-year general polytechnical secondary school leads to qualification for university attendance after a one-year period of practical work; and (8) after its implementation, attendance at the ten-year school and at least two years of vocational training will be compulsory.[34]

In the period following adoption of this law, efforts were directed towards further refining the structure of education in the GDR. The results of these efforts were contained in a draft proposal entitled "Principles for the Orientation of the Integrated Socialist Educational System," which was made available for public discussion in April, 1964. On February 25, 1965, the *Volkskammer* adopted the "Law on the Integrated Socialist Educational System."[35] This law, which represents a revolutionary change in the traditional German approach to general education, was the result of the expansive and reform-oriented educational policy carried out by the SED in the 1960's, and it remains valid in the GDR today. That aspect of the Law on the Integrated Socialist Educational System which pertains to the mandatory education of young people in the GDR provides the subject matter for this book. However, before considering this material, we will turn our attention to a brief examination of the philosophical-ideological basis of East German society since a familiarity with the basic tenets of Marxism-Leninism is essential for understanding the contemporary practice of polytechnical education in the GDR.

CHAPTER II

TOPICS IN COMMUNIST IDEOLOGY

In the socialist countries, it is openly acknowledged that education must serve society. Economic and social goals are set by the Communist Party, and the educational system is charged with explicit responsibilities in preparing youth for participation in the attainment of those goals. Communist education is, thus, carefully integrated into the fabric of society. In order to understand why children in the socialist countries are educated the way they are within a social context, a basic familiarity with the philosophy of communism is essential.

The political and socio-economic differences that exist between a nation with a tradition of Western democracy such as the United States and a socialist country such as the GDR are of sufficient scope to warrant a presentation of certain basic philosophical tenets of socialist society. For example, the calculated integration of political ideology into the educational process is an unfamiliar phenomenon to American educators. The reasons for including it in the GDR equivalent of our elementary and high school classrooms are to be found in Marxist-Leninist philosophy which forms the theoretical basis for East Germany's social, economic, and political structure.

The philosophy of Marxism-Leninism, also referred to as dialectical materialism and historical materialism, is the philosophy of communism. The basic presuppositions of this philosophy were formulated by Karl Marx (1818-1883) and further elaborated by his closest associate, Friedrich Engels (1820-1895). The most significant additions to and changes in Marxist theory, however, were the result of the work of V. I. Lenin (1870-1924), the scope of whose work was of sufficient significance to warrant joint use of the names Marx and Lenin as the appellative of the modern philosophy of communism. This developmental characteristic of early Communist philosophy has been retained by contemporary Marxism-Leninism.

Topics in Communist ideology included in this chapter have been selected for the insight that they can give towards an informed interpretation of our observations of Communist education. To this end, we shall consider (1) the Communist perception of reality, including the concepts of matter and change in dialectical materialism and the copy theory of knowledge; (2) basic tenets of Communist social and economic theory; (3) Lenin's contribution to the development of Communist philosophy; and (4) some aspects of contemporary Marxism-Leninism.

According to Marxist-Leninist philosophers, philosophical thought can be divided into the major camps of idealism and materialism. The basic difference between idealism and materialism was expressed by Friedrich Engels:

> Contrary to idealism, which asserts that only our mind really exists, and that the material world, being, Nature, exists only in our mind, in our sensations, ideas and perceptions, the Marxist materialist philosophy holds that matter, Nature, being, is an objective reality existing outside and independent of our mind; that matter is primary, since it is the source of sensations, ideas, mind, and that mind is secondary, derivative, since it is a reflection of matter, a reflection of being. . . .[1]

The approach of dialectical materialism is identified with that of science, and provides the methodological foundation for science and scientific investigation in socialist society. The laws of dialectics, or change, are fundamental to the Marxist-Leninist interpretation of reality, and the copy theory of knowledge, which will be considered later, describes the means by which this reality is transformed into human knowledge. In Marxist-Leninist ideology, the dialectic represents not only a method but is also considered to be an intrinsic property of the motion of matter. Prudence, therefore, suggests that we precede discussions of the laws of dialectics and the copy theory of knowledge with some comments on the Communist view of matter.

No distinction is made between "philosophical" and "physical" concepts of matter in dialectical materialism. The only valid view is considered to be the Leninist concept of matter which states:

> Matter is a philosophical category designating the objective reality which is given to man by his sensations, and which is copied, photographed and reflected by our sensations, while existing independently of them.[2]

The properties of matter in dialectical materialism are specified in the following theses:[3]

1. Matter is eternal, uncreated, and indestructible.

2. Matter is essentially in motion.

3. This motion in matter is essentially an upward movement, an evolution or history.

The unity of matter and motion, the second thesis, is of the utmost importance to dialectical materialism since it indicates that the

motion of matter is essentially a self-movement and, thereby, elimi-
nates the requirement of the concept of a supernatural power. This
view is in contrast to the philosophical position which holds that
matter is an absolutely static mass, which necessarily leads to the assumption of a First Mover as the original external force which set
matter into motion.[4]

The major forms of motion listed by Engels are:

> Motion in cosmic space, mechanical motion of smaller masses on a
> single celestial body, the vibration of molecules as heat, electric tension,
> magnetic polarization, chemical decomposition and combination, organic
> life up to its highest product, thought—at each given moment each indi-
> vidual atom of matter is in one or other of these forms of motion.[5]

However, dialectical materialists emphasize that

> This is not to say that each of the higher forms of motion is not al-
> ways necessarily connected with some real mechanical (external or
> molecular) motion; just as the higher forms of motion simultaneously
> also produce other forms, and just as chemical action is not possible
> without change of temperature and electric changes, organic life with-
> out mechanical, molecular, chemical, thermal, electric, etc., changes.
> But the presence of these subsidiary forms does not exhaust the essence
> of the main form in each case.[6]

The preceding discussion of the dialectical materialist conception
of matter shows the inseparability of matter and motion as a fundamental premise of Marxist-Leninist ideology. The term "motion," as
it is used in this sense, is meant to imply any kind of change. In keeping with the broadness of this concept of motion, the Marxist-
Leninist usage of the term "dialectic" includes "the general laws of
motion and development of Nature, human society and thought."[7]
Since the laws of dialectics are considered to be deduced from nature,
in Marxist-Leninist ideology they serve the dual purpose of furnish-
ing a "correct" description of reality as well as providing a method
for investigating that reality.

According to contemporary Communist interpretation, the Marxist-
Leninist dialectical process consists of the following three laws:

1. The Law of the Transition from Quantity to Quality;
2. The Law of the Unity and Conflict of Opposites; and
3. The Law of the Negation of Negation.

In essence, the Law of the Transition from Quantity to Quality
seeks to explain *how* the development of reality occurs and describes
this development as a transition from quantitative to qualitative
change:

> The development of things and phenomena in the world proceeds
> up to a certain point in the form of a gradual, merely quantitative
> change, by successive addition or subtraction. But once this quantitative
> change advances beyond the limits set by the nature of the thing in

> question, a sudden shift from quantitative to qualitative change occurs;
> the thing ceases to be what it is and becomes something else; a new
> "quality" makes its appearance.[9]

In the dialectical materialist usage, the quality of a material is determined by its inner structure. Changes in quantity—number, size, rate,
extent—have no effect on an object's quality up to the point where
further changes in quantity result in qualitative changes. At this point,
a sudden transition occurs in the form of a "leap," during which the
material's quality is changed. Not all leaps, or changes in quality, are
instantaneous, however. Since leaps characterize both evolutionary
and revolutionary forms of development, some occur over long periods
of time, including epochs.[10] In the sense that it provides a theoretical
guarantee of the continual transformation of matter, the Law of the
Transition from Quantity to Quality is fundamental to the Communist world view.

The Law of the Unity and Conflict of Opposites accounts for the
origin and nature of the process of development in dialectical materialism—it seeks to explain *why* development occurs. The law's contents are described in the following passage:

> ... dialectics holds that internal contradictions are inherent in all
> things and phenomena of Nature, for they all have their negative and
> positive sides, a past and a future, something dying away and something
> developing; and that the struggle between the old and the new, between
> that which is dying away and that which is being born, between that
> which is disappearing and that which is developing, constitutes the inter-
> nal content of the process of development, the internal content of the
> transformation of quantitative changes into qualitative changes.
>
> The dialectical method therefore holds that the process of develop-
> ment from the lower to the higher takes place not as a harmonious un-
> folding of phenomena, but as a disclosure of the contradictions inherent
> in things and phenomena, as a "struggle" of opposite tendencies which
> operate on the basis of these contradictions.[11]

The idea that motion is a "union of contradictions" is extended
in dialectical materialism beyond the concept of spatial movement
to motion of any kind. All motion in the universe has the character
of self-movement: the different elements and aspects posed in mutual
opposition to each other in all things and phenomena impels their
change and motion.[12]

The Law of the Negation of Negation may be stated briefly as
follows:

> The sudden change to a new quality, as depicted in the law of the
> transformation of quantity to quality, necessarily implies the negation
> of the previous quality. But such a negation is not the end of the matter.
> The new quality also becomes in turn the starting point for a process of

development which again leads to its negation; the first negation is
'transcended' into a new one. Thus the total rhythm of the dialectical
process is concluded by the negation of the negation.[13]

The negation of the negation does not imply immediate validation of
the past; rather, it is meant to preserve the positive aspects of previous development. Thus, dialectical development takes on the form
of an ascending spiral: "The return to the starting point is in each
case only an apparent one; the movement may well appear to be re-
verting to its starting point, but in reality it invariably regains its original position on a higher level."[14]

Dialectical materialism is both a methodology and a world view.
It deals with "the most general laws of motion, change and development in Nature, society and knowledge...."[15] In human interaction
and development, dialectical materialism means that human beings
are active rather than passive, that they are dynamically interrelated
with their social and natural environments, and that the motive force
for change and progress is provided by the antagonisms or contradictions that permeate human reality.[16] The universal applicability of
dialectical materialism, its relevance to social functioning as well as
to Nature, results in the development of a unitary conception of
existence generally known as the Communist world view. Fundamental components of Communist ideology are, therefore, the dialectical materialist concepts that matter is uncreated and indestructible and that the laws of dialectics describe an intrinsic property of
the motion of matter which is, essentially, a self-movement.

V. I. Lenin is considered to be the father of Communist education.
His work in epistemology is viewed as the ultimate authority in the
field, and his copy theory of knowledge provides the theoretical basia
for all learning in contemporary socialist society.

Two fundamental principles of Communist epistemology are: (1)
that an external world exists independently of human consciousness,
and (2) matter is knowable.[17] Matter is considered to be primary,
and consciousness, thought, and sensation are secondary. The potential for consciousness is surmised to exist "in the foundation of the
structure of matter," although, "in its well-defined form sensation is
associated only with the higher forms of matter (organic matter)."[18]

For Lenin, sensation is "the direct connection between consciousness and the external world; it is the transformation of the energy of
external excitation into a state of consciousness."[19] The human brain

is matter. Consciousness and thought are products of the brain, therefore, "mind is the highest product of matter."[20] Mind, however, is not matter, even though it is real in the sense that it exists.

Lenin considers knowledge to be a reflection, or copy of reality in the sense that operations of the external world upon the human sense organs give rise to the representations and concepts that depict, or mirror, the world outside.[21] The sensation itself is subjective, although the foundation of the sensation is objective and the relationship between them is one of correspondence; thus, ideas are derived from sensation and correspond to real objects in the external world.[22] Regarding the process by which the sensation is formed in the human brain, Lenin states:

> . . . there still remains to be investigated and reinvestigated how matter, apparently entirely devoid of sensation, is related to matter which, though composed of the same atoms (or electrons), is yet endowed with a well-defined faculty of sensation. Materialism clearly formulates the as yet unsolved prolbem and thereby stimulates the attempt to solve it, to undertake further experimental investigation.[23]

The fact that the process cannot be explained does not detract from the reality of its existence for Marxist philosophers.

Knowledge is considered to be the reflection of reality in human consciousness and, according to Lenin, it must be viewed as a process in which the mind is elevated from a state of ignorance to one of knowing, and in which there is a concomitant transformation of "things-in-themselves" into "things-for-us."[24] Lenin elaborates his view in three epistemological postulates:[25]

> 1. Things exist independently of our consciousness, independently of our perceptions, outside of us, . . .
>
> 2. There is definitely no difference in principle between the phenomenon and the thing-in-itself, and there can be no such difference. The only difference is between what is known and what is not yet known. . . .
>
> 3. In the theory of knowledge, as in every other branch of science, we must think dialectically, that is, we must not regard our knowledge as ready-made and unalterable, but must determine how *knowledge* emerges from *ignorance*, how incomplete, inexact knowledge becomes more complete and more exact *[italics in the original]*.

The acquisition of knowledge, therefore, is regarded as a dialectical process in which the human brain develops an increasingly accurate perception of reality as a result of its interaction with the external environment. The form of this interaction is *practice* and, in dialectical materialism, it is *"the foundation of the entire knowing-process, from beginning to end [italics in the original] ."*[26]

The concept of practice is fundamental to the Marxist-Leninist theory of knowledge as well as to Communist philosophy in its entirety. In Marxism-Leninism, practice is defined as tthe objective material activity by which human beings transform the phenomena and things of nature and which results in a self-transformation, or the acquisition of knowledge:

> The indispensable condition on which knowledge depends is the influence that the objects of nature and social processes exert upon man, but man can only develop his knowledge by acting, intervening in objective phenomena, and transforming them while experiencing their influence. We can understand the essence of human cognition only by deducing it from the peculiarities of this practical interaction of subject and object.
>
> . . . Man is a social and objective being and acts in an objective way. His possession of consciousness and will exerts a substantial influence on his interaction with nature. . . . Man acts with all the means at his disposal, natural and artificial, on the phenomena and things of nature, transforming them and at the same time transforming himself. *This objective material activity of man is known as practice* [italics in the original].[27]

Practice has two functions in dialectical materialism. It is the foundation of knowledge, and it serves as the criterion of truth. The basis of the first function of practice is to be found in the social character of human thought. According to the dialectical materialist point of view, knowing is a socio-historical process and, hence, it is conditioned by the development of social practice. Further, the "invisible presence" of practice in theoretical thinking is indicated by the fact that the results of thought are tested against the facts at each step in the formation of a theory. The laws of logic, by aid of which concepts are incorporated into a system, have developed in juxtaposition to the development of man's practical activity.[28]

Objective truth is considered to be "the content of human thought, as tested in practice, which is in conformity with objects, and is thus independent of the subject, man and humanity in general" in dialectical materialism.[29] According to Lenin, "man advances from subjective idea to objective truth by way of 'practice' (and technology) *[italics in the original].* "[30] The full range of objective truth is absolute truth. Man, however,

> . . . is unable to grasp—reflect—copy—Nature as a *whole*, a complete thing, in its "immediate totality," he can only approach *eternally* closer to it, by creating abstractions, concepts, laws, a scientific world picture, and so on, and so forth *[italics in the original].*[31]

Thus:

> . . . absolute truth . . . is compounded of a sum total of relative truths. Each step in the development of science adds new grains to the sum of absolute truth, but the limits of the truth of each scientific proposition are relative, now expanding, now shrinking with the growth of knowledge.[32]

There is no definite boundary between absolute and relative truth; rather, Marxist-Leninist philosophers perceive absolute and relative truth to be "dialectically interrelated in an upward movement."[33] Practice serves as the criterion for truth, since successful interactions with the external world prove the correspondence of human perception and reality.[34] Lenin incorporated these views in the dialectical materialist copy theory of knowledge which he summarized in the following terms:

> ... things exist outside us. Our perceptions and ideas are their images. Verification of these images, differentiation between true and false images, is given by practice. ...
>
> And [quoting Engels] whenever we find ourselves face to face with a failure, then we generally are not long in making out the cause that made us fail; we find that the perception upon which we acted was either incomplete and superficial, or combined with the results of other perceptions in a way not warranted by them. . .—what we call defective reasoning. So long as we take care to train our senses properly, and to keep our action within the limits prescribed by perceptions properly made and properly used, so long we shall find that the result of our action proves the conformity of our perceptions with the objective nature of the things perceived.[35]

In Communist ideology, sensation is the source of knowledge and knowledge is the reflection of objectively existing reality in the human mind. Acquiring knowledge, or learning, is the dialectical process that occurs when the human perception of reality is tested through interaction with the social and physical environments. Depending on whether or not predictions are correctly formulated, results either reinforce the original perception or lead to a new one. Learning is, thus, a continual process of perfecting the human perception of reality through practical activity. This interaction between theory and practice for the purpose of honing cognition is the essence of the polytechnic approach to learning and, as such, it is an epistemological principle that underlies all aspects of instruction in contemporary socialist education.

Marx's study of the role of dialectics in the development of human society resulted in the philosophical system known as historical materialism. A major thesis of Marx's theory of historical materialism is that the economic power in a society is controlled by those who own the means of transforming raw materials into commodities, i.e., the means of production. Political power results from economic power, so that those who control the economic power of a country also control its political power.

The individual counts mainly through his membership in a social class which has a collective unity. According to Marx, a social class acts as a unit in history and "produces its characteristic ideas and beliefs as a unit, acting under the compulsion of its place in the economic and social system."[36] Since the social classes within a society are economically competitive in their own interests, an antagonism is, according to Marx, the dynamic force of social change.

The history of culture is perceived by Marx to be the history of struggle between the dominant economic class in a given society and the masses dominated by that class. The development of human culture is viewed as an evolutionary process characterized by a succession of stages: primitive-communal, slave-owning, feudal, capitalist, socialist, and communist. According to Marx, the validity of this theory of the evolutionary development of society can be verified scientifically[37] through use of the dialectical method.

Marx viewed each stage of social development as deriving its essence, or characterization, from the relationships governing the means of production; and, the relationships governing the means of production form the structural foundation of the society. In relation to this structure, all other aspects of a society (political, legal, educational, et cetera) are part of the superstructure and derive their justification for existence from the primary structure: the relationship governing the means of production. The purpose of the superstructure, therefore, is to maintain the status quo for the class in control of the economic power.

Marx formulated his theories during the middle part of the nineteenth century against the background of the devastating exploitation of the workers by the capitalist owners of industry in England. As a consequence, he devoted much thought to the plight of man in capitalist society, in which he considered the antagonistic social classes to be the bourgeoisie and the proletariat. Marx defines the bourgeoisie as "the class of modern capitalists, owners of the means of social production and employers of wage-labor," and the proletariat as "the class of modern wage laborers who, having no means of production of their own, are reduced to selling their labor-power in order to live."[38] These classes, according to Marx, are mutually antagonistic, and this antagonism is the source of power for revolutionary change. Marx perceives the origin of this antagonism in the relationship between the proletariat and the bourgeoisie vis-à-vis the means of capitalist production.

Marx views a worker's capacity for work to be a commodity in capitalist society and, as a consequence, the worker is exposed to "all the vicissitudes of competition, to all the fluctuations of the market."[39] The worker's own labor-power is the only commodity with which he is able to barter; thus, it has an "exchange value" on the open market. The actual value of labor-power is not its real value—the productive capacity of the laborer when applied to work over a given period of time—but, rather, "the value of labor-power [exchange value] is the value of the means of subsistence necessary for the maintenance of the laborer."[40] The difference between the exchange value and the real value of the worker's labor-power appears in the form of a "surplus value," and this is the source of profit for the capitalist. The capitalist's profit is, therefore, derived from the fact that under normal conditions, the productivity of labor exceeds what is necessary to maintain the laborer.

The antagonism inherent in the social relation between the workers and the capitalist owners of the means of production becomes the source of power for revolutionary social change when it is defined and understood by the proletariat in the Marxist sense: when the proletariat becomes conscious of the economic basis of its position in the structure of capitalist society. The objective of Communist propaganda in capitalist society is, therefore, to develop the social consciousness of the proletariat for the purpose of uniting it to become an effective weapon against capitalist society. The goal is to bring about the collapse of this society.

The general position of Marx and Engels concerning the collapse of capitalist society is that it will occur during a period of prolonged depression or crisis. Although non-violent proletarian revolution is possible, Marx and Engels consider it improbable since the bourgeoisie is seen as being unwilling to yield its economic power. As a result of the collapse of capitalist society through revolution, in Marxian theory the proletariat will win the political power and will, thus, be raised to the position of the ruling class.

Marx and Engels referred to the period between capitalism and the era of communism as "a political transition period in which the state can be nothing else but *the revolutionary dictatorship of the proletariat* [italics in the original]."[41] Although no specific blueprint for this period was made, Marx and Engels envisioned it as coinciding with the existence of socio-economic classes, albeit, a dying bourgeoisie and a triumphant proletariat.[42] Marx and Engels viewed the function of the state during this period as a temporary expedient for the purpose of establishing the political control of the proletariat thereby setting the stage, as it were, for the advent of communism.

The first, or lower, phase of Communist society is termed "social-ism." Of this society, Marx stated:

> What we are dealing with here . . . is not a Communist society which
> has *developed* on its own foundations, but, on the contrary, one which
> is just emerging from capitalist society, and which therefore in all re-
> spects—economic, moral and intellectual—still bears the birthmarks of
> the old society from whose womb it sprung *[italics in the original]* .[43]

Society is still considered to be in transition during this phase in the sense that "bourgeois right," or inequality in the distribution of wealth, a characteristic of capitalism, exists in proportion to the economic transformation thus far attained. The division of labor, as well as the antithesis between mental and physical labor, remains, and society functions according to the principle: from each according to his ability, to each according to his work. Despite the fact that the means of production are no longer privately owned, but, instead, are common property of the whole society, the defects of distribution and inequality persist, giving rise to the necessity of the continued existence of the state as the dictatorship of the proletariat in socialist society.[44]

"Communism" is the term applied to the second, or higher, phase of Communist society. Marx sketched it as follows:

> In a higher phase of Communist society, when the enslaving subor-
> dination of individuals in the division of labour has disappeared, and
> with it also the antagonism between mental and physical labor; when
> labour has become not only a means of living, but itself the first neces-
> sity of life; when, along with the all-round deveieopment of individuals,
> the productive forces too have grown, and all the springs of social wealth
> are flowing more freely—it is only at that stage that it will be possible
> to pass completely beyond the narrow horizon of bourgeois rights, and
> for society to inscribe on its banners: from each according to his ability;
> to each according to his needs![45]

With the disappearance of "bourgeois rights," the existence of the state, the symbol of class society, is no longer a necessity. According to Engels, "the government of persons is replaced by the administration of things, and by conduct of processes of production. The state is not 'abolished.' *It dies out* [italics in the original] ."[46] The guiding ideal in this "new and better society" is the free development of the individual, the expansion of his intellectual and social capabilities, and the enrichment of his personality.[47] Thus, whereas in "bourgeois society, living labor [capital] is but a means to increase accumulated labor. In Communist society accumulated labor is but a means to widen, to enrich, to promote the existence of the laborer."[48]

Lenin adapted the teachings of Marx and Engels to the conditions prevalent in Russia at the turn of the century: a relatively nonindustrialized nation of exploited peasants, the great majority of which were illiterate. He determined to accomplish a proletarian revolution from the baseline of precapitalist society by eliminating, or sidestepping, the capitalist stage of social development. This adaptation, however, required some changes in and further development of Marxian theory. Leninism can, therefore, be defined as "an adaptation of Marxism to nonindustrialized economies and to societies with a prevailing peasant population."[49]

As a Marxist, Lenin was sympathetic to the condition of the proletariat; however, he had little faith in its inherent ability to develop the level of consciousness required for successful revolutionary action on its own initiative. Whereas Marx considered the seizure of economic power from the capitalist class to be an open, necessary, and, in a sense, spontaneous action on the part of the proletarian masses, Lenin's view was that the masses must be guided in their development of social consciousness by an intellectual elite, well-educated and trained in Marxist theory and tactics, whose aim was to accomplish a revolutionary change in society. The basis for Lenin's view is to be found in the contrast he made between "spontaneity" and "consciousness" as they relate to the working masses.

Lenin considered "spontaneity" to be a characteristic embodiment of the proletarian masses. Although he respected spontaneity in the sense that it was an embryonic form of proletarian consciousness and, therefore, a prerequisite for revolutionary social change, he also distrusted the inherent lack of discipline in spontaneity and its unpredictability. Lenin was, thus, led to the theory that "the spontaneous struggle of the proletariat will not become a genuine 'class struggle' until it is led by a strong organization of revolutionists," an organization which he viewed as being the embodiment of "consciousness," which can be defined as "the faculty of understanding and foresight; the ability to organize, make plans, calculate chances; the acuteness to take advantage of opportunities, to anticipate an opponent's moves and forestall them."[50] According to Lenin, the ultimate product of this consciousness was Marx's theory of historical materialism—the result of the application of the dialectical process to the history of human society—and he was convinced that a strong organization of conscious revolutionaries would be capable of developing, guiding, directing, and maneuvering the spontaneity of the masses in the desired direction of social progress.[51]

Lenin developed these ideas into the concept of the Party and its role in the development of socialist society. The ideas that he put forth in 1902 became the basis of the following definition of the Communist Party adopted by the Communist International in 1920:

> The communist party is a *part* of the working class, the most advanced, most class-conscious, and hence most revolutionary part. By a process of natural selection the communist party is formed of the best, most class-conscious, most devoted and far-sighted workers. The communist party has no interests other than the interests of the working class as a whole. The communist party is differentiated from the working class as a whole by the fact that it has a clear view of the entire historical path of the working class in its totality and is concerned, at every bend in this road, to defend the interests not of separate groups or occupations, but of the working class in its totality. The communist party is the organizational and political level which the most advanced section of the working class uses to direct the entire mass of the proletariat and the semi-proletariat along the right road *[italics in the original]*. [52]

The tasks set for the Party could be accomplished most effectively, in Lenin's view, according to his organizational concept of "democratic centralism."

The principle of democratic centralism continues to be the pivotal organizational element of contemporary Communist parties which, like the SED of the GDR, are modelled after the Communist Party of the Soviet Union (CPSU). According to the principle of democratic centralism, the higher Party bodies are elected by the lower and the Party has

> a single supreme body—the Party Congress—while between the congresses the top Party body is the Central Committee. Decisions of Party Congresses and of the Central Committee are binding on all Communists. All Party organisations are subordinated to the Party centre; the decisions and instructions of higher Party bodies are binding on all lower bodies; the minority in all organisations and their leading bodies is subordinated to the majority. Centralism also means that the lower bodies have to report to the higher ones, and that Communists have to report to their Party organisations. It also implies Party discipline and equal responsibility to the Party of all its members whatever their posts. [53]

This system of organization enabled the Party to assume a role which Joseph Stalin (1879-1953) defined on the basis of Lenin's declarations of strategy as follows:

> The highest expression of the leading role of the Party. . . is the fact that not a single important political or organizational question is decided by our soviet [governing council] and other mass organizations without guiding directions from the Party. *In this sense* it could be said that the dictatorship of the proletariat is *in essence* the 'dictatorship' of its vanguard, the 'dictatorship' of its Party, as the main guiding force of the proletariat *[italics in the original]*. [54]

Despite changes that have occurred in the Party and its tasks, its basic principles of function and organization continue to be those which Lenin formulated in 1902.[55]

The importance of Lenin's role in the development of Communist philosophy cannot be overemphasized. Within the socialist countries, his authority is equal to that of Marx and Engels, however, his influence is greater since his interpretation of their work is considered to be the only legitimate interpretation: Lenin, rather than Marx and Engels, is cited most often in doctrinal discussiona and ideological disputes.[56] As a result of the effective monopoly of power by the Party and its leadership in socialist society, the theory of socialist government is, essentially, Lenin's theory of the Communist Party and thus an appreciation of its role in socialist society is a prerequisite for understanding any aspect of that society.[57]

In the preface to the second edition of *Anti-Duehring*, Engels stated the following:

> It goes without saying that my recapitulation of mathematics and the natural sciences was undertaken in order to convince myself also in detail of what in general I was not in doubt—that in nature, amid the welter of innumerable changes, the same dialectical laws of motion force their way through as those which in history govern the apparent fortuitousness of events. . . . To me there could be no question of building the laws of dialectics into nature, but of discovering them in it and evolving them from it.[58]

From the position of dialectical materialism, Engels (1) showed that, in the final analysis, the development of natural science is determined by practical need, i.e., by production; (2) established the interdependent relationship between natural science and philosophy; (3) proved that "the metaphysical outlook has become impossible in natural science owing to the very development of the latter," that "the return to dialectics takes place unconsciously, hence contradictorily and slowly," and that dialectics "becomes an absolute necessity for natural science." Finally, Engels called on scientists to learn the conscious use of the dialectical method in the natural sciences.[59]

In the view of modern Marxist-Leninist theory, dialectical materialist philosophy is both a methodology and a world view. Its subject matter consists of "the most general laws of motion, change and development in Nature, society and knowledge. . ."; and, investigation of this subject matter results in the development of "a unitary, scientific world picture."[60] The reason, therefore, that dialectical materialism is able to provide a "closed al comprehensive world picture" is the Marxist-Leninist contention that dialectical materialism explores general laws applicable to *all* of reality; thus, the philosophy of dialectical materialism provides "a total world outlook which generalizes the findings of all the sciences."[61]

The interrelation of dialectical materialism and the natural sciences in contemporary socialist society is delineated as follows:

> Whereas the special sciences confine their inquiries to a particular portion of reality and investigate the laws operative in that field, philosophy's inquiries are directed to the laws operative in reality as a whole and in all fields in common. Hence the mutual relations of philosophy and the special sciences [do not] consist in subordination of one to the other, or in antagonism, but in a mutual interfusion and supplementation: philosophy provides the general method of scientific knowledge and a philosophical interpretation of the detailed information furnished by the sciences; the sciences supply the concrete factual material which serves philosophy as a starting point in its task of generalization.[62].

Furthermore,

> Marxist philosophy, as distinguished from preceding philosophical systems, is not a science above other sciences; rather, it is an instrument of scientific investigation, a method, penetrating all natural and social sciences, enriching itself with their attainments in the course of their development.[63]

The laws of dialectics provide the natural sciences with "general principles of operation, show them how they should approach the phenomena, and in what manner they are to investigate them"; they are, therefore, 'a tool of scientific inquiry" and a method that permeates all aspects of the natural sciences in socialist society.[64]

Marx emphasized the role of the natural sciences by pointing out that natural science "underlies all knowledge."[65] In Lenin's view, an organic link exists between science and socialism which "is expressed in the fact that socialism needs science, while science receives under socialism the optimal conditions for its development."[66] Lenin, thus, contended that the prevailing social system, rather than science itself, is the determining factor of the social purpose of scientific research as well as its orientation, pace of development, and the utilization of its results.[67] According to contemporary Marxist-Leninist theory, the significance of science for socialist society is that

> socialism is in acute need of science by its very nature. It can demonstrate its superiority only if it is supported by the most progressive achievements of the human intellect and if these achievements are given extensive opportunity for realization.[68]

Science has two major functions in socialist society: economic and educative. The economic function of science lies in its utilization for effective economic development of socialist economies: Lenin claimed that "labor productivity is in the final analysis the most important, the principal element for achieving the victory of the new social system."[69] The educative function of science is found in its "daily and extensive employment" for the purpose of forming "harmoniously developed" socialist individuals.[70]

Basic to the educative function of science in socialist society is the claim that Marxism-Leninism is unique in its ability to provide a correct scientific explanation of the human environment, including its physical and social aspects. Emphasis on the scientific nature of communism creates a special attitude of alliance with science among Marxist-Leninists in general.

The integral relation between science's educative function and its function in the economic development of socialist society is evident in the Marxist-Leninist definition of science which states that "science is a socially conditioned process of cognition of the objective world, results of which comprise a continuously developing system of knowledge, utilized by society to transform reality."[71] In a broad sense, the transformation of reality in Marxism-Leninism refers to the human ability to apply scientific knowledge in order to change the physical and social environment for the purpose of improving the human condition. In a narrower sense, it refers to the realization of Communist economic and social goals through the economic transformation of socialist society as a result of the application of science to the processes of production.

Contemporary Marxist-Leninist philosophy is firmly based in the work of Marx, Engels, and Lenin. The patterns of thought that originated in their work have persisted to the present time and there is no indication that changes in basic Communist theory or pattern of thought will change in the foreseeable future.[72]

Certain doctrines which form an essential part of Marxism-Leninism are: (1) matter is all that exists; (2) reality is essentially dialectical; (3) the triumph of communism is inevitable; (4) aims of communism coincide with the aims of working mankind; and (5) the Party is the vanguard of mankind and will lead it to communism.[73]

Marxist-Leninist philosophy considers human society to be an aspect of the material world and, therefore, it is governed by the laws of dialectics. Human society, however, is seen as being qualitatively different from the rest of the material world and, as such, it has specific laws governing its development. The Marxist-Leninist laws of social development are objective and independent of the will and consciousness of human beings, although human beings can use their knowledge of these laws to achieve their own ends in the same ways that physical laws are used. According to the world view of Marxism-Leninism, the interests of mankind are inherent in Communist philosophy and, therefore, correct use of the laws of social development of dialectical materialism will ultimately lead to the achievement of communism which is considered by Marxist-Leninists to be the highest level of humanitarian social development attainable."[74]

The following official definition of communism was adopted by the Twenty-second Congress of the CPSU which met in Moscow during October-November, 1961:

> Communism is a classless social system with one form of public ownership of the means of production and full social equality of all members of society; under it, the all-round development of people will be accompanied by the growth of the productive forces through continuous progress in science and technology; all the springs of cooperative wealth will flow more abundantly, and the great principle, "From each according to his ability, to each according to his needs," will be implemented. Communism is a highly organized society of free, socially conscious working people in which public self-government will be established, a society in which labor for the good of society will become the prime vital requirement of everyone, a necessity recognized by one and all, and the ability of each person will be employed to the greatest benefit of the people.[75]

This version of rhe definition of communism is in essential agreement with Marx's definition; although the emphasis has been added that the means by which this stage of social evolution is to be achieved is through the further development of science and technology.

The Communist Party is the most authoritative guide in the process of social development, according to the Marxist-Leninist world view, since it represents the objective truth of human society in its laws, morality, and philosophy.[76] As Lenin emphasized:

> Communism would not be communism without the notion of the dictatorship of the proletariat. The Party is the vanguard of the proletariat leading mankind forward and guarding humanity along the road of its future progressive development.[77]

Current Marxist-Leninist theory attributes similarities that exist in the superstructures of contemporary capitalist and socialist societies, as well as in their traits, norms, and morals, to an overlap of remnants of the previous, capitalist, stage of social evolution in socialist society. According to Communist theory, the level of development of the societal superstructure lags behind that of the base as a result of the fact that the base changes at a more rapid rate than does the superstructure.[78]

The development of the superstructure of a socialist society such
as the GDR is directed and led by the Communist Party for the purpose of creating socio-economic conditions favorable for the attainment of communism. From the Marxist-Leninist point of view, the
ideological work of the Party is an increasingly powerful factor in
this development. Ideology, in Marxism-Leninism, is defined as

> a system of views and ideas: political, legal, moral, aesthetic, religious,
> and philosophical. It is part of the superstructure and as such reflects in
> the final analysis economic relations. The struggle of class interests in a
> society with antagonistic classes corresponds to the ideological struggle.
> Ideology may be a true or a false, a scientific or an unscientific, reflec-
> tion of reality.[79]

According to Communist theory, dialectical materialism is the only
valid philosophy. Dialectical materialism is also an ideology and, since
ideology is considered to be a form of philosophy, Marxist-Leninists
make no distinction between them.[80]

The goal of ideological work in socialist society is to develop a
"new man" who is free of the "deceit, cruelty, and prejudices of the
old, bourgeois world," and whose character is an alloy of such qualities as

> dedication to the Communist cause, socialist patriotism and interna-
> tionalism, conscientious labour, a high sense of public duty, vigorous
> social and political activity, intolerance of exploitation and oppression
> and of national and racial prejudices and class solidarity with the work-
> ing people of all countries.[81]

The Communist Party, therefore, calls for

> the education of the population as a whole in the spirit of scientific
> communism and strives to ensure that all working people fully under-
> stand the course and perspectives of world development, that they take
> a correct view of international and domestic events and consciously build
> their life on Communist lines. Communist ideas and Communist deeds
> should blend organically in the behavior of every person and in the acti-
> vities of all collectives and organizations.[82]

Special importance is attached to the "molding" of the rising
generation.[83] The primary focus for the development of the "new
[Communist] man" in socialist society is during the period of compulsory education where attainment of this mentality is a basic goal
permeating all areas of instruction. The extent to which ideological
training plays a role in the educational process is apparent in a recent
statement by Margot Honecker, Minister of Education of the GDR,
in which she outlined the responsibility of the schools in developing
a Communist morality in young East Germans:

> . . . we look upon the education of youth to develop a Communist
> morality as a complex process of political and ideological, mental, phy-
> sical, and aesthetic education, education in the spirit of patriotism and
> internationalism—as education through work and the influence of a col-
> lective. It is only in this complex process that the character of young

people can be moulded and brought out, including their political and ideological convictions, faithfulness to the cause of the working class, implacability vis-à-vis the class enemy, as well as a zest for knowledge, social activity, a strong will and sense of duty, respect for life, for working man and older people, courage, sincerity, comradeliness, helpfulness, modesty, and reliability. We must instill such traits into girls and boys so that every one of them is able to live up to the demands of life and the tasks arising from work and the struggle today and in the future.[84]

CHAPTER III

EDUCATING EAST GERMAN YOUTH

The Law on the Integrated Socialist Educational System informs us that the GDR has entered a new, socialist stage of cultural evolution and that the most important aims in the construction of socialism are "to master the technological revolution, to develop the national economy of the German Democratic Republic, and to increase production and labour productivity on the basis of the highest standard of science and technology...."[1] These aims, in turn, provide the basis for formulating the general objectives of the integrated socialist educational system of the GDR:

> The socialist educational system makes an essential contribution to enabling the citizens to shape the socialist society, to master the technological revolution, and to participate in the development of socialist democracy. It imparts an up-to-date general education and a high level of special training, and at the same time develops traits of character in accordance with the spirit of the principles of socialist morality. The socialist educational system enables them to perform good work as citizens, to keep on learning, to be active in society, to take part in planning, to take on responsibility, to live in a healthy manner, to use their leisure time sensibly, to go in for sports, and to appreciate the arts.[2]

The underlying purpose of education in any society is to imbue the younger generation with that society's aims and to provide them with adequate knowledge and skills for its maintenance and further development. In the West, we make education do this in a fairly anarchical way, with the result that the relation between educational objectives and social goals is clouded. In the socialist countries, the purpose of educational planning is to support the social and economic goals of socialist society, a relation that permeates all aspects of the instruction process. How is education controlled in a socialist society such as the GDR? How are East German economic and social objectives reflected in the compulsory educational program of the GDR? These and other questions will be treated in the following pages as we develop a picture of the general education of young people in a contemporary socialist society.

[38]

All GDR citizens are guaranteed equal rights to a free education within the integrated socialist education system. The fundamental components of this system are: (1) institutions for pre-school education; (2) the ten-year general polytechnic secondary school; (3) institutions for vocational training; (4) educational institutions leading to higher education; (5) engineering institutes and technical schools; (6) universities and other institutions of higher learning; and (7) institutions for the training and further training of working people. In addition, special schools exist for children who are physically or mentally handicapped.

The ten-year general polytechnic secondary school is the compulsory school, requiring the attendance of all young East Germans between the ages of six and sixteen. Specialized education, pursued after completion of the period of compulsory education, offers opportunities for the attainment of specialized knowledge and the acquisition of vocational skills.

The integrated educational system is fluid in the sense that, after completing the ten-year general polytechnic secondary school, an individual has the option of proceeding by various paths—depending in differing degree on individual inclination, intellectual capabilities, and national occupational requirements—through the educational structure's stages to the highest educational institutions, the universities and colleges (Fig. 3-1).

Administration and planning for the integrated socialist educational system is centrally controlled and hierarchically structured. Central decisions regarding all aspects of national educational policy are made at the highest level of this structure, and directions for their detailed implementation are passed down through consecutive hierarchical levels to the level of local educational administration; thus, the uniformity and coordinated control of national educational policy is assured. Recommendations for changes in educational policy and assessments for funding and facilities are made according to a reverse process, whereby recommendations and assessments made at local levels are submitted to successively higher levels of the administrative structure for collation with final decisions being made at the highest administrative level on the basis of recommendations made by immediately subordinate administrative organs.

The GDR Council of Ministers, the chief executive organ of the State, is at the highest level of the hierarchical structure for educational administration and planning. Its prime function in the area of education is to make ultimate decisions regarding national educational policy and to ensure that the level of development and educational excellence is adequate to permit the successful fulfillment of the GDR's long-term and annual economic plans.

FIGURE 3-1

THE INTEGRATED SOCIALIST EDUCATIONAL SYSTEM
IN THE GDR[3]

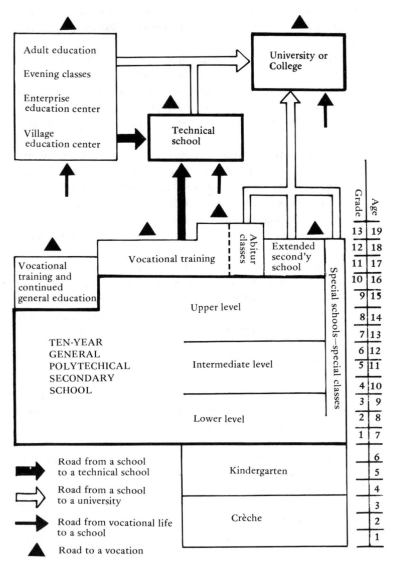

Among the state organs directly responsible to the Council of Ministers for matters concerning education are: (1) the Ministry of Education, which is responsible for the control of kindergartens for children between the ages of three and six years, the ten-year general polytechnical secondary schools, the development of programs of instruction and curricula, and teacher training; (2) the Ministry for Higher and Technical Education, responsible for the control and planning of technical schools and other institutions of higher education, including the universities; (3) the Ministry of Health, which supervises the creches attended by children under three years of age; and (4) city, county, and district councils, which are popularly elected bodies concerned with the administrative functioning of the schools and, therefore, responsible for the management of school services, provision and maintenance of buildings and equipment, and provision of school inspectors, supervision, and administration.[4]

The basic ideological and pedagogical control of the ten-year general polytechnical secondary schools is applied by the Ministry of Education through the curricula, teaching plans, and textbooks which it confirms for uniform use throughout the country, as well as through salaries and organizational and legal directives which are valid for the entire country. Textbooks for all schools are generally prepared by a group of experts, and final manuscripts pass through a complicated system of control and approval prior to publication by state pedagogical publishing houses. Curricula are also produced by teams of experts including educators, teachers, and subject-area specialists.[5]

The major function of the Ministry of Education is to develop the theoretical foundation of education in the compulsory schools. Educational research for the ten-year general polytechnical secondary schools is the domain of the Academy of Pedagogical Sciences of the GDR, which is located in Berlin and is responsible to the Ministry of Education for

> advancing the scientific development of educational practices, studying and evaluating the practical experiences of the best teachers and schools, planning and executing educational research, and coordinating the research plans of universities and teachers' colleges.[6]

Aims of educational research in the GDR include the development of more effective methods of implementing current programs, the improvement of conditions of instruction, and the strengthening of the all-round development of socialist personalities.[7]

The central control of education in the GDR refers to the domination of education by the highest-ranking governmental agency, the GDR Council of Ministers. In reality, however, the function of the

the Council of Ministers is that of administering, or putting into practice, the policy decisions made at the highest level of the Communist Party of the GDR, the Political Bureau of the Central Committee of the SED.

The Political Bureau of the Central Committee of the SED functions within GDR society as the contemporary construct of Lenin's concept of the vanguard of the proletariat. Its decisions, are, therefore, considered to be made on the highest authority by Marxist-Leninists. The control of the GDR Council of Ministers by the Political Bureau of the SED ensures the Marxist-Leninist orientation of education in the GDR. The contemporary status of compulsory education in the GDR can, thus, be regarded as a Communist statement concerning the most effective basic education currently possible for the development of productive socialist citizens in the technological age.

The integrated socialist educational system of the GDR—the nucleus of which is the ten-year general polytechnical secondary school—is integrally related to the planning and management of the national economy and the process of scientific-technological development. By 1980, for example, the GDR expects to increase the number of people with scientific training working in the national economy by 250 percent and the number of scientists and technicians for 350 percent over the 1967 levels.[8] In this regard, the basic tasks of providing the necessary and appropriate fundamental education, of selecting youth who exhibit exceptional talent in science and science-related areas, and of persuading other youth to enter science-related vocations are the responsibility of the ten-year general polytechnical secondary school of the GDR. The means by which the general schools are expected to fulfill their responsibilities vis-à-vis the scientific-technological aspect of national economic planning are, fundamentally, through the program of science education and related polytechnical instruction. In the remaining pages of this chapter, we will examine the way in which the GDR's national social and economic objectives have been translated into a comprehensive program for compulsory education.

The name "ten-year general polytechnical secondary school" is the general term applied to the compulsory schools attended by GDR youth starting at the age of six and continuing until satisfactory completion of the academic requirements of mandatory education has been accomplished. The title "Ten-Year General Polytechnical Secondary School" is also the individual name of the 5,067 general schools distributed throughout the GDR (*Fig. 3-2*).

FIGURE 3-2

Map of the GDR Showing the Distribution of Ten-Year General
Polytechnical Secondary Schools According to District in 1975[9]

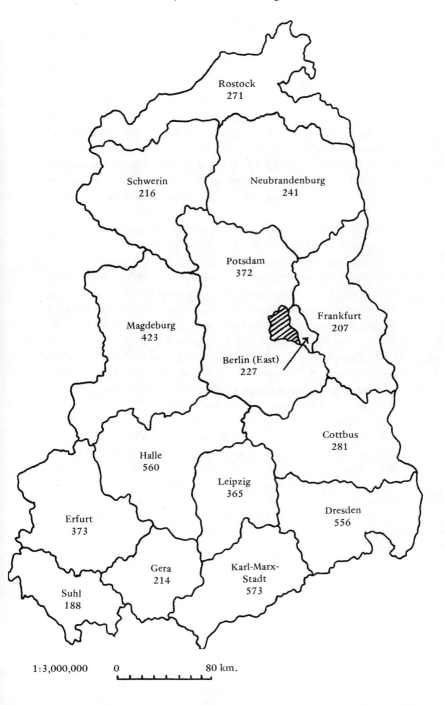

Rostock
271

Schwerin
216

Neubrandenburg
241

Potsdam
372

Magdeburg
423

Frankfurt
207

Berlin (East)
227

Cottbus
281

Halle
560

Leipzig
365

Dresden
556

Erfurt
373

Gera
214

Karl-Marx-
Stadt
573

Suhl
188

1:3,000,000   0   80 km.

The ten-year general polytechnical secondary schools are attended by all children "whose legal guardians have their residence, or are continually staying, in the German Democratic Republic" and who are physically and psychologically capable of undertaking the mandatory academic work.[10] Two groups of children not educated in these schools include those who attend special schools for physically and psychologically handicapped children, and students who, as a consequence of exceptional talent, attend specialized schools in art, music, sports, science and mathematics, or languages, et cetera. Both groups, however, are comparatively small in number. In 1975, for example, the enrollment of students in the special schools represented 3 percent of the total 2,578,782 students attending the ten-year general polytechnical secondary schools, or 71,104. Although the number of students attending the specialized schools for gifted children is unpublished, it is considered to be negligible in comparison to the number of students attending the general schools.[11]

In addition to these two groups, there are two groups of students who acquire compulsory education through the eighth year in the general schools but complete it concurrently with vocational education during a three-year period in a vocational school, or are selected to continue academic studies in the four-year extended general polytechnical secondary schools (hereafter referred to as extended secondary schools) which are comprised of grades 9 through 12.

The number of students in the first group, those who leave the general schools at the end of the eighth year for the purpose of entering vocational training, has decreased continually since 1965 to 241,065, or 8.4 percent of the total number of students attending the eighth grade of the general schools in the GDR.[12] . Students who are selected to leave the general schools at the end of the eighth year for the purpose of continuing their academic education in the extended secondary schools are chosen on the basis of scholastic achievement, tentative choice of vocation, Marxist-Leninist conviction, and space available. Although a high scholastic record is the general requirement for admission to the extended secondary school, students who intend to pursue careers as military officers are admitted on a preferential basis with lower academic credentials than otherwise required. On the basis of existing statistics it is estimated that approximately 8 percent of all eighth grade students in the general schools are admitted to the extended secondary school at the start of the ninth grade for the purpose of preparing for university study and acquiring the *Abitur* which qualifies them for admission to a university.[13] (*Table 3-1*).

TABLE 3-1

Distribution of Students in the Ten-Year General
Polytechnical Secondary School (GP), the Special Schools,
and the Extended Polytechnical Secondary School (EP)
for 1975[14]

GP, Special Schools, and EP
   Number of Schools 5,921
   Number of Students 2,697,740
   Students per class 25.3

GP (including grades 9 and 10 of the EP)
   Number of Schools 5,067
   Number of Students 2,578,782
   Students per class 26.2

Special Schools
   Number of Schools 569
   Number of Students 71,104
   Students per class 26.2

EP (grades 11 and 12)
   Number of Schools 285
   Number of Students 47,854
   Students per class 12.0

The number of students attending the Special Schools
   compared to the number attending the GP 3%

The percentage of 8th grade students in the GP
   who entered the 9th grade 91.6

The percentage of the total number of students in the
   10th grade of the GP and EP who entered the
   11th grade of the EP 12

The number of students in the EP who took the
   examination for the *Abitur* 24,490

Options taken by students who have completed the 10th
   grade of the general and extended polytechnical
   secondary schools in 1976:*
      (1) vocational training for two year period 83%
      (2) vocational and continued academic training
         for three-year period 5%
      (3) entry into the 11th grade 12%

* Information given by Herr Grosser, an official in the GDR Ministry for
Education, on March 16, 1977.

The great majority of young East Germans—over 80 percent in
1975—complete the period of compulsory education in the ten-year
general polytechnical secondary school. Options available upon successful conclusion of this period are: (1) training for vocational qualification at a vocational school for a period of two years; (2) entering a three-year school in which vocational qualification and academic

preparation for the *Abitur* are obtained concurrently, and (3) continuing academic work in the extended secondary school. The last option, however, is seldom taken since the majority of qualified students are selected for the extended secondary school during the 8th grade. The frequency with which these options were recently chosen is indicated by the following statistics: of the total number of students who completed the 10th grade of the general and extended polytechnical secondary schools in 1976, 83 percent began a two-year period of vocational training, 5 percent entered the three-year program of vocational training with preparation for the *Abitur*, and 12 percent—a figure comprised largely of those students selected for academic work in the 8th grade—continued academic studies in the 11th grade of the extended polytechnical secondary school. It is, therefore, apparent that the majority of GDR youth begin vocational training upon completion of the period of compulsory education; and although further training is encouraged for the purpose of obtaining higher vocational qualifications, for most young people in the GDR completion of the ten-year general polytechnical secondary school represents the conclusion of formal academic study.

Since the period of compulsory education represents the singular experience that most GDR citizens have with formal academic instruction, it also represents a period of intensive effort on the part of the national government to[15]

1. establish a high-level, modern socialist general education as a prerequisite for creative activity in production and all other areas of society and as a prerequisite for the people's mastery of the scientific-technological revolution;

2. establish the ideology of the working class [Marxism-Leninism] as the prerequisite for conscious socialist action in the interest of the working class and all workers in the GDR, i.e., to develop an identification with the ideas of socialism in the young people;

3. equip [the nation's youth] with the political-moral characteristics and behavior patterns that distinguish revolutionary fighters for the working class.

Thus, the period of compulsory education in the GDR is utilized to develop a nation of youth who are fervently patriotic to the socialist state and who are equipped in their education and training to contribute productively to its economic development.

In order to accomplish these objectives, the Central Committee of the SED set forth the following tasks for the general schools in conjunction with the Eighth Party Congress of the SED:[16]

1. to structure the contents [of learning] in the general schools so that they correspond to the requirements and conditions of a mature socialist society;

2. to provide the youth with a high-level, scientific general education and to achieve a high level of effectiveness in their socialist upbringing;

3. to prepare youth ever more thoroughly for life and work within the context of socialist society and to further intensify the polytechnical character of the general schools;

4. to develop the creative forces and abilities of youth on the basis of solid knowledge and understanding;

5. to furnish youth with high-level ethical-moral and aesthetic-cultural values; and

6. to educate and train them in the spirit of a socialist world view to become conscious socialist citizens who are faithful to the ideas of socialism and who maintain themselves as patriots and [Communist] internationalists.

These Marxist-Leninist concepts of education form the foundation and the philosophic orientation for the program of compulsory education in the ten-year general polytechnical secondary school of the GDR.

The educational program of the general schools is divided into three stages: the primary stage, which includes grades 1 through 3; the intermediate stage, which includes grades 4 through 6; and the secondary stage, which includes grades 7 through 10 (*Appendix A*).

Areas of compulsory education are comprised of (1) the social sciences, German language and literature, and the arts and music; (2) mathematics; (3) the natural sciences; (4) polytechnical education and training; (5) the Russian language; and (6) sports. The subjects taught in these areas and their level of presentation conform to the cognitive development of the child at each grade level (*Table 3-2*).

In the primary stage of compulsory education, approximately 50 percent of instruction time is allotted for the study of the German language and its literature and an average of 10 percent allotted for drawing and music. Neither the social sciences nor the natural sciences form a distinctive part of the curriculum during this stage, but, rather, are included in German language and literature instruction as *Heimatkunde*, the introductory study of local history and topography. Mathematics represents 24 percent of formal instruction time in the primary stage, whereas polytechnical instruction (in the form of industrial arts and gardening) and sports comprise 16 percent of the curriculum. Russian language study is not part of the educational program during the primary stage.

TABLE 3-2

Timetable for the Ten-Year General Polytechnical Secondary School[17]

Subject	Grade 1 1st ½	2nd ½	2	3	4	5	6	7	8	9	10
German	11	10	12	14	14	7	6	5	5	3	4
Russian	-	-	-	-	-	6	5	3	3	3	3
Mathematics	5	5	6	6	6	6	6	6	4	5	4
Physics	-	-	-	-	-	-	3	2	2	3	3
Astronomy	-	-	-	-	-	-	-	-	-	-	1
Chemistry	-	-	-	-	-	-	-	2	4	2	2
Biology	-	-	-	-	-	2	2	1	2	2	2
Geography	-	-	-	-	-	2	2	2	2	1	2
Industrial Arts	1	1	1	1	2	2	2	-	-	-	-
Gardening	-	1	1	1	1	-	-	-	-	-	-
Polytechnical Instruction :	-	-	-	-	-	-	-	4	4	5	5
Introduction to Socialist Production	-	-	-	-	-	-	-	(1)	(1)	(2)	(2)
Technical Drawing	-	-	-	-	-	-	-	(1)	(1)	-	-
Productive Work	-	-	-	-	-	-	-	(2)	(2)	(3)	(3)
History	-	-	-	-	-	1	2	2	2	2	2
Civics	-	-	-	-	-	-	-	1	1	1	2
Drawing	1	1	1	1	2	1	1	1	1	1	-
Music	1	1	1	2	1	1	1	1	1	1	1
Sport	2	2	2	2	3	3	3	2	2	2	2
Hours per week	*21*	*21*	*24*	*27*	*29*	*31*	*33*	*32*	*33*	*31*	*33*
2nd Foreign Language, optional	-	-	-	-	-	-	-	3	3	3	2
Needlework, optional	-	-	-	-	1	1	-	-	-	-	-
Total number of hours per week	*21*	*21*	*24*	*27*	*30*	*32*	*33*	*35*	*36*	*34*	*35*

At the intermediate level of compulsory education, grades 4 through 6, 44 percent of formal instruction, on the average, is devoted to history, geography, German language and literature, drawing, and music, with 29 percent allotted for instruction in the German language and literature. Mathematics forms 19 percent of the curriculum; the natural sciences of biology and physics, which are introduced in the fifth and sixth grades, respectively, comprise an average of 7 percent; polytechnical education and training in the form of industrial arts and gardening form 8 percent; the Russian language, introduced in the fifth grade, forms 12 percent; and sports form 10 percent of the total educational program.

The secondary stage of compulsory education is marked by the intensification of the polytechnical education and training area of instruction. The subjects entitled "Introduction to Socialist Production," "Technical Drawing," and "Productive Work" form a course complex which is undertaken one day each week in school-associated industries for the purpose of learning the productive processes associated with the industries and of doing productive work under the guidance of skilled workers and technicians. (*Cf. below, Chapter IV*) Polytechnical education and training forms an average of 14 percent of the total educational program at this stage; the area of the social sciences, German language and literature, drawing, and music, an average of 34 percent; mathematics, 15 percent; the Russian language, 9 percent; and sports, 6 percent of the total curriculum. During the secondary stage, 22 percent of the general school educational program is devoted to the natural sciences: biology, physics, and chemistry are taught during each of the grades 7 through 10 and the subject of astronomy is added in the tenth grade (*Appendix B*).

Consideration of the five areas which form the educational program of the ten-year general polytechnical secondary school indicates that:

1. The proportion of time devoted to formal instruction in geography, the social sciences, German language and literature, the arts, and music decreases from 60 percent during the primary educational stage to 44 percent at the intermediate stage and 34 percent at the secondary stage.

2. The quantity of time spent on formal instruction in mathematics decreases from the primary stage through the secondary stage; however, the decrease from 24 percent at the primary stage to 19 percent at the intermediate and 15 percent at the secondary stage is not substantial.

3. The portion of the total currriculum devoted to formal instruction in the natural sciences shows a substantial increase from no specific science subjects during the primary stage to 7 percent in the intermediate stage and 22 percent, or over one-fifth of the compulsory curriculum, during the secondary stage.

4. The time devoted to polytechnical education and training increases considerably from 8 percent during the primary and intermediate stages to 14 percent during the secondary stage.

5. Study of the Russian language increases from a zero contribution in the primary stage curriculum to a 12 percent contribution in the intermediate stage curriculum and shows a slight decrease to 9 percent of the secondary stage curriculum.

6. The portion of the total general school curriculum devoted to sports increases slightly from 8 percent in the primary stage to 10 percent during the intermediate stage, but then decreases to 6 percent during the secondary stage (see Fig. 3-3).

In analyzing these trends, it is important to note the influence of the interpenetration and overlap of disciplinary areas which is an essential characteristic of the educational program in the general schools. Thus, for example, although the academic area that includes the social sciences shows a proportionate decrease from the primary through the secondary stage of the educational program, the practical application of the social sciences and their implications form a significant aspect of the polytechnical education and training course complex as well as of the subject of physical geography. Also, the overall exposure of students to science in the secondary stage is greater than the 22 percent contribution made by the natural science subjects at that level of the educational program, since a major aspect of the polytechnical education and training course complex involves practical application of the theories of natural science to the processes of production in industry and agriculture.

At the secondary stage of compulsory education in the GDR, an average of 36 percent of the school curriculum is devoted to studying science and technology. Fifty-one percent of the educational program at this level is allotted to the study of natural science, polytechnical subjects, and mathematics. The percentage of the educational program devoted to science and science-related subjects during the last four years of compulsory education reflects the significance of science and technology in contemporary GDR society.

The underlying purpose of East German education is, as previously noted, to contribute to the further development of socialism and the GDR national economy. This realization cannot be overemphasized as we try to understand the current status of compulsory education in the GDR. Since science and its applications in modern industry are the basis of economic development, the Communist leadership of the GDR ascribes the greatest importance to education in

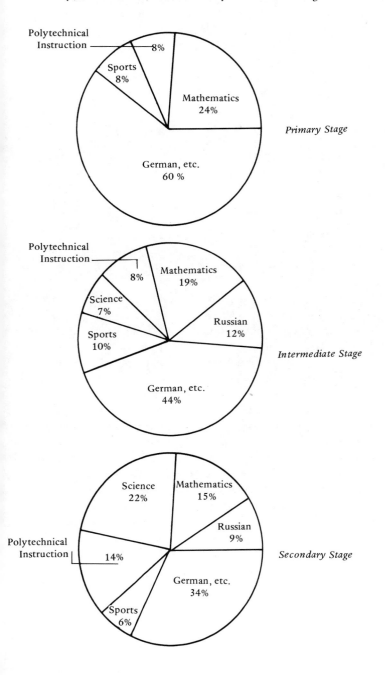

FIGURE 3-3

Apportionment of Formal Instruction Time for the
Major Instructional Areas during the
Primary, Intermediate, and Secondary Educational Stages[18]

Polytechnical
Instruction —— 8%

Sports
8%

Mathematics
24%

Primary Stage

German, etc.
60 %

Polytechnical
Instruction ——

8%

Mathematics
19%

Science
7%

Russian
12%

Sports
10%

Intermediate Stage

German, etc.
44%

Science
22%

Mathematics
15%

Russian
9%

Polytechnical
Instruction

14%

Secondary Stage

German, etc.
34%

Sports
6%

these areas. At the Ninth Party Congress of the SED which met in Berlin from May 18—22, 1976, it was stated:

> Science and knowledge stand in an inseparable relationship. Scientific knowledge is a broad foundation for the education and training for the younger generation and for the qualification of all workers.[19]

The GDR's planned scientific-technological development and the Communist conviction that Marxism-Leninism has a scientific basis indicate the predominant position held by science in GDR society and, hence, in its schools. By the time East German young people complete the ten-year period of compulsory education, they have studied biology for five years, physics for four years, chemistry for three years, and astronomy for one year. Additionally, they have had a year of physical geology in the ninth grade under the heading of geography. The mathematics program provides them with an average of one hour of mathematics instruction each day over the ten-year period. During the first five years of this program, the emphasis is on basic arithmetic; however, geometry is introduced in the second grade and culminates in plane and solid geometry in the sixth, seventh, and eighth grades. Algebra is studied in grades 6 through 9, and the compulsory mathematics program concludes with a year of trigonometry in the tenth grade.

Naturally, a major function of courses in the natural sciences and related subjects is to impart fundamental knowledge of the specialized subject matter. However, in socialist society, science education also has the more general functions of contributing to the development of a Marxist-Leninist world view and of demonstrating the relationship between science knowledge and technology. Since the relationship between science instruction and political education as well as the intensity of the instructional relationship between science and technology are unfamiliar aspects of compulsory education outside of the socialist countries, they bear further comment.

The interfusion of Marxist-Leninist ideology and science in the science curriculum of the ten-year general polytechnical secondary school is a logical consequence of the relationship between science and philosophy in dialectical materialism.[20] The task of Marxism-Leninism in relation to the sciences is that of guiding empirical inquiry:

> ... experience, practice, is the decisive test even in theoretical matters, but to methodology, i.e., to theoretical reflection, there falls the extremely important task of filling in the gaps left in experience and empirical science.[21]

At the level of compulsory education, GDR educators contend that the interfusion of science knowledge and Marxist-Leninist ideology leads to the development of a scientific view of life and a scientific philosophy in young people. In their view, Marxist-Leninist concepts of matter, the laws of motion and of development, et cetera, aid in the scientific clarification of basic natural phenomena and enable students to intellectually unify science and the natural and social, the total, environment. By conveying the basic knowledge of Marxism-Leninism, science education is viewed as making a significant contribution to the philosophical training of GDR youth, thus enabling them to exist harmoniously in socialist society and to live in correspondence with the goals and interests of that society. The role of Communist ideology in the learning process is described as follows:

> In courses and lessons based on and consistently involving the relevant sciences, children in the GDR are taught to think logically and accurately, ask about causes and the laws involved, and substantiate theses. It is only natural that they learn to apply these methods not only in dealing with problems in mathematics and the natural sciences but also in investigating social processes and evaluating political opinions and measures. For that purpose Marxism-Leninism serves them as a scientific world outlook, which has again and again proved its usefulness as a basis from which reality can be understood and mastered, which stands the test of being applied to practice as the criterion of truth and which constantly develops.
>
> We make no secret of the fact that in our schools the children are educated for socialism in the world outlook of Marxism-Leninism, and as conscious citizens.[22]

The interrelation of Marxist-Leninist philosophy and science education is expressed in the tasks of science education in GDR compulsory schools. A reading of these tasks is important since they serve to illustrate the specialized and general aspects of science learning in socialist compulsory education. They are:[23]

1. to provide a basic natural science education through examination of the fundamental laws of natural science;

2. to contribute significantly to the development of intellectual capabilities through presentation and practical application of the methods by which natural science knowledge is acquired, including instruction in experimental procedures, the formation of theories, model representations, et cetera;

3. to establish the foundation of a broad and fundamental technical education through continual application of the fundamental knowledge of the natural sciences to the solution of technical problems, through the analysis of technical development with reference to its basis in natural science, and, finally, through the systematic examination of the natural science foundation of modern technological development; and

4. to provide an essential contribution to the formation of social-ist consciousness in GDR youth and to contribute to their upbring-ing in the world outlook of the working class through political-ideo-logical generalization of basic natural science knowledge as well as through presentation of the political consquences of the mastery of the scientific-technological revolution.

The fourth task is a statement of the role of political education in science learning. Six major areas of Marxist-Leninist ideology have been defined by GDR educators for the purpose of integrating poli-tical education into the process of science instruction. They include (1) basic dialectical materialist orientation and attitude towards the human environment, (2) insight into social relationships and laws, (3) socialist norms of behavior and morality, (4) insights into and knowledge of the materialist dialectic, (5) insights into the theory of knowledge, and (6) insights into the methodology of dialectical materialism.[24]

The specialized aspect of science learning, of course, is emphasized in GDR schools, and young people are expected to master a wide range of science knowledge by the time they complete the ten-year period of compulsory education. However, they are also expected to acquire an understanding of the general nature of science and its ap-plicability to daily existence. In this sense, GDR educators have made significant inroads towards making science education relevant to life in socialist society.

Lenin's view best sums up the approach to science stressed in the GDR's ten-year general polytechnic secondary school. He attacked views of science as pure knowledge and demanded "that science in [socialist society] not remain a dead letter or fad phrase. . . . That science genuinely enter our flesh and blood, that it be transformed into a component of our lives, fully and genuinely."[25] This recom-mendation has been made operative in GDR compulsory education through the correlation between technical activity, political educa-tion, and science instruction which exemplifies the polytechnic approach to learning.

According to J. D. Bernal, 'Science is . . . complete only when its results are transformed into practice. . . . For this reason, the evalua-tion and examination of science cannot be separated from techno-logy."[26] In the view of educators in the GDR and Communist edu-cators in general, the close interrelation between science subject mat-ter and technology provides an excellent pedagogical opportunity to intensify learning in both areas.

The basis of this position is that a knowledge of the laws and processes of natural science is fundamental to acquiring an effective understanding of modern technology. On the other hand, the natural sciences can be fully understood by students only when they are related to technology. In the process of applying the laws of natural science to a variety of relevant technical situations during the polytechnical instruction portion of the school curriculum, GDR educators contend that students will intensify their science understanding, develop science-associated skills and abilities, and further develop their scientific interests and attitudes. Learning outcomes aspired to as a result of the close correlation between the subject matter of science and technology include attainment of (1) a strong interest in, or love for science, (2) pleasure in discovery and investigation, and (3) the ability to recognize the scientific problems in technological situations and to ask relevant questions creatively.[27]

The specialized knowledge of scientific laws and processes provided by science instruction furnishes the scientific basis required for understanding modern production processes. By integrating information concerning the application of science in industry into the process of science instruction, East German educators hope to develop student appreciation of the vital role of science in the development of modern technology. This approach also imparts knowledge of the specialized branches of science that have developed as a result of the interrelation between science and technology and the technology and the technological application of the natural sciences. Additionally, by utilizing technical material in science instruction, a familiarization with relationships that exist between the natural sciences and production processes is promoted, including (1) the production process as the origin of questions in the natural sciences, (2) science as the effective principle and agent for technical explanation, and (3) science as the model and challenge for technical realization.[28]

CHAPTER IV

THE POLYTECHNICAL APPROACH TO LEARNING: A UNITY OF THEORY AND PRACTICE

According to Marxist-Leninist philosophers, antagonism between mental and physical labor is a trait of capitalist society that overlaps the transition to socialism; therefore, antagonism between mental and physical labor exists in socialist society as a vestige of capitalism. Its origin in capitalist society is seen in the exploitation of factory workers by the mental workers who manage them. In contrast to the lack of esteem for physical labor that Marx and Engels perceived in capitalist society, they regarded manual labor as a factor of major significance in the process of human development. For Marx and Engels, labor "is the prime basic condition for all human existence, and this to such an extent that, in a sense, we have to say that labour created man himself."[1]

Resolution of the antagonism between mental and physical labor is a major task of educators in the GDR and other socialist countries for two reasons. First, a sizeable and continually expanding work force of skilled and semi-skilled laborers is a primary requirement for the successful fulfillment of plans for the future economic development of the GDR. In order to muster the requisite number of laborers without reaping consequential disaffection within their ranks, it is deemed necessary to develop an appreciation for physical labor. A second reason is to be found in the Marxist-Leninist thesis that antagonism between mental and physical labor will not exist in the future Communist society where physical labor will have been transformed from a burden into a primary necessity of life. The onus, therefore, is on contemporary socialist society to develop this Communist attitude toward labor. As a result of the control exercised over education in the GDR by the policy making level of the SED, the compulsory ten-year general polytechnical secondary school is the most effective arena for resolving the antagonism between physical and mental labor.

[56]

A fundamental problem of physical labor as it relates to the growth of modern industry is that of the worker whose job becomes obsolete as a result of automation. Marx recognized the dangerous potential inherent in this problem for the worker and outlined its solution in the following terms:

> ... Modern Industry ... through its catastrophes imposes the necessity of recognising, as a fundamental law of production, variation of work, consequently fitness of the labourer for varied work, consequently, the greatest possible development of his varied aptitudes. It becomes a question of life and death for society to adapt the mode of production to the normal functioning of this law. Modern Industry, indeed, compels society, under penalty of death, to replace the detail-worker of today, crippled by life-long repetition of one and the same trivial operation, and thus reduced to the mere fragment of a man, by the fully developed individual, fit for a variety of labours, ready to face any change of production, and to whom the different social functions he performs are but so many modes of giving free scope to his own natural and acquired powers.
>
> One step already spontaneously taken towards effecting this revolution is the establishment of technical and agricultural schools ... in which the children of the working men receive some little instruction in technology and in the practical handling of the various implements of labour.... there can be no doubt that when the working class comes into power, as inevitably it must, technical instruction, both theoretical and practical, will take its proper place in the working-class schools.[2]

The concept of combining productive labor with instruction is the basis of the approach taken by educators in the GDR and other socialist countries for the purpose of developing a Communist attitude towards labor in youth. The manifestation of this approach is the polytechnization of compulsory education in socialist society. Communist educators contend that by exposing all youth to polytechnical education—to practical, productive experiences in industry and agriculture integrated into the overall educational program—during the compulsory school years, they will develop a respect for manual labor and its products.

Although the origin of the polytechnical concept of education is generally sought in the work of utopian socialists, Communist educators attribute the first valid systematic statement of the theory of polytechnical education to Marx and Engels:

> In our view, there are three aspects of education: first, intellectual education, second: physical development training..., third: polytechnical training, which imparts the general scientific principles of all production processes and, simultaneously initiates the child and the young person in the practical use and manipulation of the elementary instruments of all industries.[3]

Educators in the GDR consider this concept of the elements of education to be contemporarily valid and they view their task to be that of applying it creatively to present levels of development in the areas of production, science, and technology.

Nadezhda Krupskaya, the wife of Lenin and a figure of primary importance in the establishment of Communist educational theory, is given major credit for development of the concept of polytechnical education within the framework of Marxism-Leninism. The following account of her views regarding the integration of polytechnical instruction into the educational program of the schools provides a synopsis of the implementation of polytechnical training in the contemporary general schools of the GDR:

> [Krupskaya] proposed a complete re-examination of the school curriculum and syllabuses, with a view of ensuring that all children have the possibility of reaching the highest level of scientific and technological knowledge integrated into their training in manual skills. In the preparation of syllabuses, research workers and technologists should come to the aid of teachers in discarding out-of-date material and working out the polytechnical approach. She saw the possibility of a new subject of study, "organization of work," acting as the connecting link between the school curriculum and the political-economic society in which the school functions. Productive work by the children should not be carried on under school auspices in isolation from the outside world, but in factories and farms side by side with the workers normally active there, whose participation would serve as an aid in the extension of the polytechnic principle to the adult community and in the involvement of working adults in the whole educational process.
>
> Krupskaya stressed that the productive work of the children should not be too highly specialized: experience in the factory should be so organized as to lead to an understanding of the function of each department within the total effort of the factory and of the role of the factory in the total economy of the area and of the country. Productive work should be both industrial and agricultural; it should be explicitly related to the content of classroom work; it should lead to an understanding of chemical as well as mechanical production; and it should be a training in initiative and intellectual adaptability as well as in manual skill and scientific knowledge.[4]

Today, in the compulsory schools of the GDR, polytechnical education is an attitude that permeates all subject areas by relating theoretical learning to practical activity in daily life and a course complex that seeks to provide young people with opportunities for observing and participating in the technological application of scientific theories in industry. The polytechnical approach to learning is an expression of the Marxist-Leninist thesis that knowledge is acquired through a dialectical interaction between theory and practice. Since Marxism-Leninism purports to furnish the theoretical basis for understanding all of reality, the polytechnical approach to compulsory education provides Communist policy makers with a means of relating observations and experiences in the social and physical environments to their bases in Communist theory via classroom instruction. Ideally, there is a constant dialectical interplay between the surrounding environment and the school so that the school, rather than being isolated from the environment, is in a continuum with it. This interaction is most pronounced in the polytechnical courses of the upper grades where strong efforts are made to relate technology and production processes and the observations and experiences of students to their bases in natural science theory and in Marxist-Leninist social and economic theory.

On January 17, 1979, *Neues Deutschland*, the major East German newspaper published daily by the SED, carried the following article under the headline, "Production Tasks in Polytechnical Centrums":

> 70,200 girls and boys from the 7th though the 10th grades receive polytechnical instruction in 85 industrial learning centers in the [GDR] capitol. 900 of them attend the polytechnical centrum that developed as a result of cooperation between VEB Men's Clothing "Progress" and other factories [VEB, or *Volkseigener Betrieb*, is a designation that is literally translated as "Peoples' Own Industry"]. As early as 1958, 140 pupils from the 7th and 8th grades began the "Day of Instruction in Production" in a workshop in which they could become familiar with the fundamentals of metal working. Today, pupils participate in production. Among other things, they manufacture crowns and slide mechanisms for [garden] sun umbrellas and ball bearings for children's bicycles. Girls from the 9th and 10th grades do finishing work on men's jackets. Boys work in shipping and technical divisions.
>
> VEB Bergmann-Borsig, which gegan [polytechnical] instruction 17 years ago with 600 students, is training 2,200 girls and boys this year. The curriculum promotes the acquisition of basic skills and knowledge of the metal working [industry]. 7th and 8th graders work at the side of 60 . . . workers who assist them. In the Polytechnical Centrum of the Electrical Apparatus-Works Treptow, pupils have achieved noteworthy productive results on the basis of this curriculum.
>
> 2,140 girls and boys from the 11th and 12th grades of the extended secondary schools do scientific-practical work in 74 factories and institutions. Thus, they can apply their theoretical knowledge of the natural sciences creatively. For example, students from the EOS [Extended Secondary School] "Alexander von Humboldt" last year developed a frequency counter with their [factory] "instructors" which was commissioned by the VEB Funkwerk Koepenick and it will be exhibited at the "Fair of the Masters of Tomorrow." The instrument is characterized by extremely small dimensions and a direct indicator of frequencies up to 120 megacycles. With it, a savings of 25,000 Marks over previous models can be attained.[5]

Questions that arise concern the organization of polytechnical instruction and its integration in the total process of education. Obviously, young people are learning in factories as well as contributing to the productive output of these establishments.

Current educational theory in the GDR stresses three major functions of polytechnical education and training: it is pre-vocational training; it is an essential aspect of general education; and it establishes the interrelation between instruction, the productive work of the students, and modern industrial production.[6] As an aspect of general education, the function of polytechnical education is to provide the intellectual foundation required for understanding the fundamental areas of contemporary human existence—such as modern industrial production, labor, and man-made environments—for the purpose of controlling and utilizing them for human advantage.

Major objectives of polytechnical eduction in the GDR are to introduce students to the intellectual functions of technology, to qualify them for technical activity, to provide them with vocational preparation, and to guide their socialist personality development.[7] By introducing students to the intellectual foundations of technollogy, GDR educators intend that students obtain technical work experience and work knowledge as well as an introduction to the scientific basis of production processes. In a broader sense, however, students are expected to acquire a polytechnical horizon including knowledge of the main branches of production and the relations between them, the geographical distribution of the nation's major industries and the sources of raw materials, and the role of the local area and of the GDR within the socialist economic system.[8]

Polytechnical instruction is vocational preparation in the sense that it provides young East Germans with a broad range of technical training so that they will have sufficient knowledge, skills, and abilities to aid them in dealing with problems related to job obsolescence. Students are also expected to gain an understanding of their "human role in the process of social production"—that is, to acquire a Communist conviction—through interaction with factory workers, through studying the theoretical foundations of industrial production processes, and through the practical experience of applying this knowledge by doing productive work in industry.[9]

Polytechnical instruction in the ten-year general polytechnical secondary school is composed of two stages (*Figure 4-1*). The first stage, grades 1 through 6, consists of manual training and gardening instruction. Manual training, which involves one hour of formal in-instruction per week in grades 1 through 3 and two hours per week

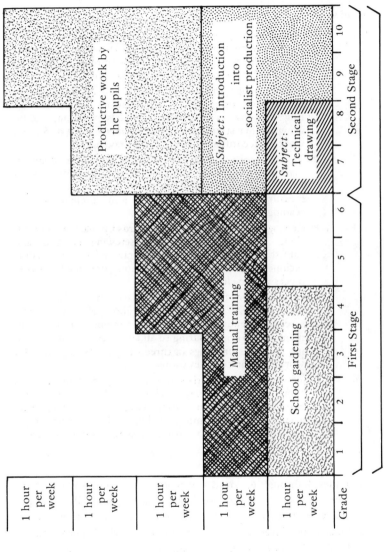

FIGURE 4-1: Two Stages of Polytechnical Education and Training in the Ten-Year General Polytechnical Secondary School[10]

| Grade | 1 | 2 | 3 | 4 | 5 | 6 | 7 | 8 | 9 | 10 |

1 hour per week

1 hour per week

1 hour per week

1 hour per week

1 hour per week

Productive work by the pupils

Subject: Introduction into socialist production

Subject: Technical drawing

Manual training

School gardening

First Stage

Second Stage

Ten Year General Polytechnical School

TABLE 4-1

Manual Training in Grades 1 Through 6[11]

Grade	Activities
1	Simple processing of paper, cardboard, and plastic foil by marking with templates, cutting with scissors, and connecting different parts by glueing; measuring patterns prepared by the teacher to an accuracy of 1 cm.;
2	Processing paper, cardboard, boards, and artificial leather by marking, using a ruler and drawing compasses; cutting with scissors and connecting parts by glueing and by using leather straps; measuring to an accuracy of 5 mm., working according to models and drawings;
3	Processing paper, boards, and flexible plastic materials by marking, using ruler and triangle, cutting with scissors and hand-lever shears, joining by glueing and sewing; measuring to an accuracy of 1 mm., preparation and reading of simple drawings;
4	Processing wood and wood fiberboards by marking, sawing, filing, drilling, glueing, nailing, screwing, painting, and varnishing; measuring to an accuracy of 1 mm., reading technical drawings in two dimensions, drawing flat workpieces in one elevation;
5	Processing wood, fiberboards, and plastic materials by marking, shearing, sawing, filing, drilling, glueing, nailing, screwing, bending, folding, and engraving; surface treatment of wood; measuring to an accuracy of 1 mm., reading technical drawings in three dimensions, drawing flat workpieces in two elevations;
6	Processing plastic materials and metals by marking, sawing, filing, drilling, glueing, welding plastic foil, screwing, bending, folding, embossing, swaging; measuring to an accuracy of 1/10 mm., reading and preparing simple drawings of flat and rotationally symmetric workpieces.

in grades 4 through 6, consists of work with paper, plastics, straw, leather, and wood. Instruction takes place in specially equipped school workshops (see *Table 4-1*). Two major aspects of manual training at this level are to introduce pupils to the fundamentals of technological work with materials and to provide them with simple basics of technical design and shaping related to elementary concepts of machine and electrical engineering.[12]

Formal instruction in gardening entails one hour per week during the first four grades and usually involves the care of a large kitchen garden in which vegetables are grown for the school or the canteen of a school-associated factory, but can also include simple jobs in local parks. These activities are designed to aid young students in their understanding of nature and to prepare them for biology instruction through experiences such as making tests on soil structures and becoming familiar with growth factors, fertilization, and different cultivating measures.[13] In general, the purpose of polytechnical instruction at this stage is to introduce children to technical and economic matters, to develop their work skills and their ability for technical drawing, and to survey the domestic economy.[14]

Grades 7 through 10 comprise the second stage of polytechnical education and training in the GDR. At this stage, all polytechnical instruction takes place in school-associated industries or training centers one day per week. This day is referred to as the *Unterrichtstag in der sozialistischen Produktion* (UTP), or "The Day of Instruction in Socialist Production." In grades 7 and 8, polytechnical instruction consists of four hours of instruction per week: one hour per week in each of the courses entitled "Introduction to Socialist Production" and "Technical Drawing," and two hours per week in "Productive Work." In the ninth and tenth grades, five hours per week are devoted to polytechnical instruction; three of these are devoted to "Productive Work" and two to "Introduction to Socialist Production" (*see Table 4-1*). The type of practical work done by the students during this second stage depends on the facilities available in local industries. Availability of local industrial facilties also determines, to a considerable extent, the area of technical specialization and influences the content of technological theory, the polytechnic orientation of the natural science courses, technical drawing, and the subject matter of "Introduction to Socialist Production" in the ninth grade.[15]

To a considerable extent, Introduction to Socialist Production is taught according to a uniform teaching program so that subject matter contents are essentially the same whether the predominant environment of the school is rural-agricultural or urban-industrial, with the exception of grade 9 where content is directly related to available local industrial facilities. Instruction for this subject occurs in specially equipped rooms in the factory rather than in a school classroom.[16]

In grade 7, students are introduced to the factory and basic manufacturing processes such as cutting, metal forming, joining, and surface refinement. They acquire knowledge concerning the scientific and technological aspects of their work as well as information concerning the profitability of using various work materials. In the eighth and first part of the ninth grades, students learn the construction and function of machines and their elements, the technological utilization of machines, and their efficiency in the various branches of the national economy. The second half of the ninth grade is devoted to learning the "foundations of production of the socialist enterprise." Here, students learn about the essential production tasks of the enterprise, the use of materials and energy, the main stages of the production process, the measures to increase productive efficiency in factories, the tasks of skilled workers and supervisors, and the interrelations of workers as "owners and masters of production." The curriculum for the tenth grade is devoted to electrical engineering and includes the significance of electrical engineering for the economy of the GDR, introductory material concerning the technology of measuring and testing, and heavy- and weak-current technology.[17]

At all grade levels, efforts are presently being made to give more consideration to the individual interests and needs of boys and girls in technology, to develop a greater variety of student activities and higher standards of student performance, and to promote a closer interrelation between this subject and the teaching of mathematics, science, and the productive work of the students inside the factory.[18]

The curriculum for Productive Work differs for schools located in rural-agricultural environments and those located in predominantly urban-industrial settings. In grades 7 and 8, instruction takes place in the training and production places of the school-associated enterprises, and the work program is varied depending on the enterprise: "operation, material, work pieces, machine parts come from the finishing and repair programme of the enterprise concerned."[19] During the seventh and eighth grades, subject contents of this course include the processing of raw materials, both manually and with the aid of simple machines, and simple assembling and disassembling processes. The agricultural variant of the course includes basic skills and work knowledge of the processes of agricultural production.

Special techniques have been developed which enable students to manufacture products of good quality and high use value. For example, seventh and eighth graders who are doing their productive work at the *VEB Transformatorenwerk* Berlin make elements for electric lawnmowers and various components for transformers. They also participate in repair plans and make modest contributions to the factory's innovative development. At an agricultural enterprise near Meissen, eighth grade pupils tend 150 calves. Their activities include determining the amount of feed (water, concentrates, roughage, and forage), preparing and providing water and feed for various age groups of the calves, cleaning the calf pen and work utensils that are used, observing the animals through health checks, undertaking certain disease prevention measures, and participating in weighing the animals and keeping their documents.[20]

In the ninth and tenth grades, the curriculum for "Productive Work" is further differentiated into the ten major industrial categories of the industrial-agricultural complex of the GDR. Again, the availability of local industrial facilities is the factor which determines the type of productive work that students will be involved in. The ten major industrial categories into which the ninth and tenth grade curriculum for "Productive Work" is differentiated are: the engineering industry, the electrical industry, the construction industry, agriculture, the chemical industry, the textile industry, the woodworking industry, the leather industry, the clothing industry, and the maintenance of farm machinery. Productive work in each of these categories includes experiences in (1) the "operation, supervision and maintenance of machine tools or other machines doing mechanical work," (2) "helping in maintenance work or the carrying out of complex assembly work," and (3) in "the carrying out of specific operations depending on the branch of industry or agriculture concerned."[21]

Currently, about 75 per cent of the ninth and tenth graders work directly in factories or enterprises, and the remaining 25 per cent do their productive work in production departments set up for students in factory or factory-associated polytechnical centers. In contrast to the seventh and eighth graders, their work is characterized by a more acute sense of responsibility resulting from their increased involvement in enterprise affairs and the higher level of development of their skills and knowledge. For example, in VEB Carl Zeiss Jena and its affiliated enterprises, 11,000 students produced products valued at about 3 million marks in 1975. They also raised the yearly productive output of these enterprises by 18 percent, while at the same time lowering the percentage of rejects and parts that required reworking from 7 to between 3 and 4 percent.[22]

A series of optional productive work curricula have been developed for the purpose of catering to the individual interests of students and in which they can participate on an extra-curricular basis. Thus, after-school interest groups in productive work exist for automotive engineering, radio engineering equipment, repair of durable consumer goods, cooking-serving-housekeeping, the health system, wholesome nutrition, the building industry (interior work), and socialist environmental protection. These programs, together with those for extracurricular activities in the areas of science and technology, are an essential aspect of polytechnical training in the GDR's ten-year general polytechnical secondary schools.[23]

In general, by the time young East Germans complete the tenth grade, they have acquired a solid practical knowledge as well as skills and good working habits and, as a result of their experiences in production enterprises, they have no illusions concerning the adult "world" of daily work. Polytechnical instruction, thus, provides them with a good basis for future vocational training; a factor of importance, since approximately 90 percent of all students who have completed the tenth grade in the GDR enter a two or three-year period of vocational training.

The Polytechnical Centum VEB Secura-Werke, located on East Berlin's Rungestrasse, is a place where seventh through tenth grade students from schools in the surrounding area go for polytechnical instruction. It is maintained and run by the VEB Secura-Werke, an affiliate of VEB Kombinat Zentronik with headquarters located some distance away on the Chauseestrasse, which manufactures equipment related to computer technology. The Centrum itself is a relatively narrow, six-story structure situated in a courtyard behind a row of drab-looking buildings and, on this cold and wet afternoon in late November, the predominant visual impression was grey.

Permission to visit polytechnical centers such as the one affiliated with the Secura-Werke is given only guardedly by East German officials. The opportunity to visit this Centrum represents the first time an American has been granted official permission to visit a Polytechnical Centrum and observe students during the "Day of Instruction in Socialist Production."

The director of the Centrum, Dr. Laube, greeted me at the entrance and ushered me up five flights of stairs to his office, where we were joined by a representative from the *Haus des Lehrers*, or House of the Teachers, in East Berlin. Within minutes of meeting these people and instructors and students, the cold greyness of the outside faded and was replaced instead with an atmosphere of enthusiasm and friendliness.

Prior to visiting the work rooms and observing polytechnical in-instruction, Dr. Laube gave an introductory description of the Centrum and its functions. The Polytechnical Centrum is a place where upper grade students receive polytechnical instruction and training in the courses entitled "Introduction to Socialist Production," "Technical Drawing," and seventh and eighth grade "Productive Work." A total of 1,622 students from the seventh through tenth grades attend the Centrum coming from six polytechnical secondary schools, one special school for deaf children and youth, and one extended secondary school. The Centrum's lower-floor classrooms are reserved for instructing all seventh through tenth graders in the subject "Introduction to Socialist Production." The upper-floor *Kabinette*, or work rooms, are the places in which seventh and eighth graders and some ninth grade students do productive work. Other ninth graders and all higher grade students complete productive work requirements at the main site of VEB Secura-Werke on the Chauseestrasse and at its branches in other parts of the city.

The program in polytechnical training and instruction is integrated with the school curriculum and arranged so that students attend courses in the "Introduction to Socialist Production" and 'Productive Work" on alternate weeks, thus alternating theoretical instruction and practical training. In the eighth and ninth grades, four hours per week are allotted for this instruction and six hours are spent in polytechnical classrooms each week in the ninth and tenth grades.

At present, the annual cost of maintaining this Centrum is 420,000 marks, a cost which is met by thirteen companies. In keeping with the premise that positive psychological effects, such as motivation and the development of interest, accrue when work is done for a purpose, students annually produce 200,000 marks worth of products at the Polytechnical Centrum VEB Secura-Werke. Of the total goods produced, 75 percent are produced directly for the Secura-Werke and the remaining 25 percent for other companies. Products produced for other companies are included in the instructional program by the Secura-Werke so that students have the opportunity for acquiring the full range of skills and abilities called for by the curriculum of the ten-year general polytechnical secondary school.

Each of the seventh grade *Kabinette* accommodate up to eighteen students at one time. The work room I visited was equipped to give seventh graders fundamental experiences in metal working. The current project was to produce metal holders for attaching flower boxes to the balconies of apartment buildings and houses. The work places in the *Kabinet* were equipped with vises, drill presses, shearing machines, and metal saws. Students spend about one-third of their time working at the drill presses and two-thirds of their time at the vises. Productive work classes are instructed by one or two *Lehrmeister* or *Ingenieurpaedagogen*, who generally come from the ranks of factory workers and who have continued their education for the purpose of qualifying as instructors for "Productive Work" courses.

The *Lehrmeister* responsible for this seventh grade *Kabinet* was a pleasant and enthusiastic former machinist. Among his comments was one concerning the attitudes of girls and boys in the productive work classes. According to his experience, girls initially tend to have a somewhat greater fear of machines than do the boys. Later, however, they have a similar degree of readiness to work at machines. Thus, for example, the instructor referred to the case of an *Arbeitsgemeinschaft*, or interest group in productive work, which he leads for students as an extra-curricular activity. Of the six young people participating in this group, four are girls. None of the girls intend to enter technical vocations, but participate in this work activity because they enjoy it.

The *Lehrmeister* stressed that considerable emphasis is placed on industrial safety in the productive work classes and that prior to each class session, students are briefed on pertinent safety procedures. All polytechnical instructors are required to complete a training program in fundamental industrial safety and first aid. In this connection, the *Lehrmeister* commented on the fact that each student is required to wear a net over his hair in the work room. In deference to individual taste, students have recently been permitted to wear their own choice of hair cover rather than the uniform grey-mesh caps required previously, as long as they conform to current standards of safety.

Prior to leaving the *Kabinet*, the *Lehrmeister* remarked that students derive emotional benefits from working on the drill presses—they enjoy working on them and so this activity has an uplifting effect.

Some of the machinery in the ninth grade work room was more complex than that of the seventh grade room. The *Kabinet* was cheerfully decorated with colorful "wall newspapers" and plants and was equipped with drill presses and lathes. The lathe is a more complicated piece of equipment than the drill press, and I was informed that girls, since they tend to be initially inhibited when confronted with complex equipment, are generally assigned to the drill presses at the beginning of the school year and later advance to the lathes.

An important motivational factor for the students is that the work they do is utilized for the national economy. Young people instructed in this *Kabinet* produce parts for the Secura-Werke. In order to develop their sense of responsibility, each machine has a tag attached to it informing students of the machine's original monetary value. Work instructions are provided for students in the form of a technical drawing of the part they are to produce and its specifications and the ninth graders are expected to do their work with a minimum of assistance from the instructor. Although they are not paid for the products they produce, good work is recognized and groups of students or individuals with the best results can win bonuses.

The first eighth grade *Kabinet* I visited was set up for assembly-type work involving both individual and assembly-line construction. The students were producing parts for a calculating machine manufactured by the Secura-Werke. In order to give these eighth graders a sense of involvement and a feeling of shared repsonsibility for the overall production of this calculator, each student was provided with a work sheet which contained an illustration of the final product. An arrow connected a schematic drawing of the part they were manufacturing to its location on the final product and information was given concerning the part's function in the whole.

Fifteen students and three adults, the head of this *Kabinet* and two *Lehrmeister*, were present on this day. Production goals for the work period were determined by the students on the basis of information concerning work norms for the job that they were doing as established by employees (TAN) and student work norms (SAN) for the same job. The student manufacturing process included quality inspection of the finished parts. Knowledge of the entire process of producing a part is obtained by rotation to new positions on the assembly line after working at the same place for two class sessions.

In the second eighth grade *Kabinet*, students were manufacturing a drive shaft. The director of the Centrum commented that this is the only place in the Secura-Werke where this part is produced, and the students' recognition of this fact has had a positive effect on their attitude towards work and on the development of their social responsibility. In fact, the maturity of young people in both classes was impressive. There was a sense of goodnatured seriousness about the way in which they approached their work and interacted with one another, and there was no hint of artificiality in their behavior to indicate that they had been instructed to maintain themselves in a special way for the sake of visitors.

In the hallway outside the student work rooms, Dr. Laube directed my attention to a wall on which were posted pictures of recent winners and the current status of the "Socialist Student Competition" for the VEB Secura-Werke in a variety of competitive categories. Results are based on three major criteria which are evaluated after each class period. Criteria include quality of workmanship, the quantity of products successfully completed, and observation of safety regulations. During the first few lessons of a new school year at the Polytechnical Centrum, students discuss and formulate goals in these areas and, for the purposes of determining the competitive results, their actual work is measured against the goals set.

Other areas of competition are solidarity or *Solidaritaet*, wall newspapers, and the *Messe der Meister von Morgen*. Students can offer productive work which they do after school and during vacations for socialist "solidarity." A money estimate is made of this work and the financial yield is then transferred to a "solidarity account." Ultimately, the money is utilized to promote the cause of communism by providing assistance to underdeveloped nations or by helping to obtain the release of political prisoners who have been imprisoned in other countries because of their activities. Students who do this kind of work receive a certificate in recognition of their participation in the solidarity movement and, at regular intervals, an entire class receives a certificate indicating how much its members have contributed to the solidarity account. As in other competitive areas, winners generally receive a bonus which they can either divide among the group or use to pay for a group outing or other activity.

Wall newspapers are outlays of news and information of relevance to the students of a given class which are displayed on a wall in the *Kabinet* in a generally colorful and interest-provoking way. Each class develops its own wall newspaper, and competition between classes is based on such factors as the quantity and currency of the news and informaton and its manner of presentation. The *Messe der Meister von Morgen* (MMM), literally, the "Fair of the Masters of Tomorrow," provides young East Germans with the opportunity for displaying their creative talents, individually or in groups, in areas of scientific and technological construction and development within the context of a science and technology fair for young people. The overall purpose of all of these competitions is that of motivating young people to work accurately and efficiently within the collective working environment that characterizes socialist production enterprises.

According to Dr. Laube, educational outcomes for polytechnical courses are difficult to assess due to the short time that a given class of students is in the Centrum and the large total number of students who attend classes at the Centrum each week. However, student interaction is promoted through requirements of the work process and the independence, or self-reliance, of the students is encouraged particularly through activities such as applying industrial safety procedures, et cetera.

Coordination and cooperation between the Centrum and its associated schools is an area that needs further development. The same applies to many other factory-school associaions throughout the GDR. For example, although the courses entitled "Introduction to Socialist Production" are taught at the Polytechnical Centrum VEB Secura-Werke, the teachers involved are responsible to the respective directors of the participating schools, a situation which causes their cooperation with the Centrum's director to be a matter of good will. Formerly, these classes were taught at one location for an entire city district, or *Stadbezirk*, but now they are decentralized according to polytechnical centers such as that operated by the Secura-Werke.

An organization that has been developed for the purpose of coordinating between a polytechnical centrum, its associated schools, and course instructors for "Introduction to Socialist Production" is the *Polytechnische Bereit*, or polytechnical advisory council. Such councils are comprised of representatives from the schools, the companies involved, the polytechnical centrum, and they can also include interested parents. The factory, however, bears the major responsibility for polytechnical education; *Lehrmeister*, for example, are factory employees.

In order to expedite contact between the Polytechnical Centrum VEB Secura-Werke, its associated schools, and the instructors for "Introduction to Socialist Production," Dr. Laube has initiated a program in which *Lehrmeister* are assigned to maintain contact with each of the schools for purposes of communicating on subjects such as student achievement and problem areas. To facilitate this communication, a responsible student from each school is assigned to carry a "shuttle" copybook in which messages can be conveyed between school and Centrum personnel.

Are vocational interests aroused in young people as a result of their polytechnical education and training at the Centrum? In answer to this question, Dr. Laube stated that the Secura-Werke tries to fill as many vocational training positions as possible with students who have had their polytechnical instruction at the Centrum so that the trainees are familiar with the industry and will not be disappointed in their work after completing vocational training. Naturally, this is not always possible. However, Dr. Laube stated that more than 50 percent of the deaf students who attend this Polytechnical Centrum receive subsequent vocational training positions at the Secura-Werke.

The visit was over and I thanked my host for a most interesting and informative afternoon. The integration of learning and work that I had observed was a compelling demonstration of how compulsory education can be made relevant for school-aged teenagers. The earnest enthusiasm evident in the Centrum's workrooms indicates that young people can enjoy involvement in socially productive activities. In this context, positive personality characteristics are reinforced and the gap between school and work is bridged. Clearly, this is an approach to the education of young people that merits international attention.

CHAPTER V

INSTRUCTION IN A SOCIALIST CLASSROOM

We next turn our attention to the process of instruction in a socialist classroom. A generalized description of classroom procedure is facilitated by the uniformity that prevails in all aspects of education related to the ten-year general polytechnical secondary school. For example, as we have noted previously, all curricula currently being used in these schools have been centrally planned and developed in the Academy of Pedagogical Sciences of the GDR. The curricula are treated as laws and, in essence, teachers are legally bound to teach the subject matter outlined in them. Textbooks have been designed to correlate with the curricula for each subject for each grade level and their use in the general schools is mandatory. Subject-specific methods books describe and elaborate on the methodological bases for teaching these subjects as they are perceived by esteemed GDR pedagogical scientists. Further uniformity in teaching methodology is attained through the use of books entitled *Unterrichtshilfen* published for specific subjects at each grade level for the purpose of providing teachers with a daily guide to the presentation of subject matter. Instructional aids, available for all subjects, are listed and identified according to whether their use is obligatory or optional in an official book published under the auspices of the Ministry of Education of the GDR. Against this background of educational uniformity, differences exist mainly in the variation of teacher personality and the physical plants of the schools.

The Act on the Integrated Socialist Educational System of 1965 contains the following statements pertaining to curricula, textbooks, and teaching aids for the ten-year general polytechnical secondary school:[1]

> (1) Instruction shall be given according to state curricula which ensure the scientific and systematic character of teaching. The curricula stipulate the basic content of education for a longer period. The Ministry of Education shall ensure that the curricula are worked out in team work by educationists, teachers, and scientists of other fields.

> (2) Textbooks and teaching aids shall be in accord with the content of the curricula.

(3) Scientific materials and papers on teaching methods shall be made available to the teachers, helping them to plan, prepare, and carry through instruction on a high level.

(4) Curricula and textbooks shall be confirmed by the Ministry of Education. The Ministry of Education shall approve the teaching aids.

As with all other parts of the Act, or Law, on the Integrated Socialist Educational System, school administrators and teachers are legally bound to adhere to its precepts. Thus, for example, the curricula in current use are regarded as laws upon which all instruction and evaluation of learning outcomes are based.[2]

In January, 1963, the Sixth Party Congress of the SED called for the transformation of the then-existing GDR educational system to an integrated socialist education system as an essential aspect of the entire further development of socialist society in the GDR. In this connection, the following three suggestions were made at the Congress:[3]

1. It was recognized that "the educational system changes its contents, organizational forms and methods with the development of society, science, technology, state and culture;" therefore, the contents of education must be constantly re-examined to enable the school to keep "pace with the life of society" so that the school retains its usefulness for society as well as for the individual.

2. The manner in which "general and vocational education could be brought together more closely with retained primacy of general education and without effacing the specific nature of each branch of education" must be considered.

3. A reconsideration of the methodological organization of instruction was necessary. "New ways had to be found, above all, to intensify instruction and to achieve greater results."

In March, 1963, the GDR Council of Ministers complied with a proposal of the SED's Sixth Party Congress and established the "State Commission for the Organization of the Integrated Socialist Educational System" The members of the commission "represented all sciences and all spheres of life of importance for the educational system"; their assignment was to consider all problems surrounding the further development of the educational system of the GDR.[4] The culmination of these efforts led to the ratification of the Law on the Integrated Socialist Educational System by the *Volkskammer*, or People's Chamber, of the GDR on February 25, 1965, and its implementation began in the 1965-66 school year.

A major task of implementation of the Law was the development of new curricula for all areas of instruction in the ten-year general polytechnical secondary school. Under instructions from the Ministry of Education, the German Central Pedagogical Institute—which developed into the Academy of Pedagogical Science of the GDR in September, 1970—constructed the required curricula with the assistance of nearly "3,000 experts involved in educational scientific or practical work, in other sciences or activities. . . ."[5] In each case, curriculum modifications were based on:[6]

1. the exigencies of further development and completion of socialist society in the German Democratic Republic;

2. the consequences stemming from the nature of socialist democracy and the role of socialist ideology in socialist society in the GDR;

3. the requirements of [the] scientific-technological revolution; [and];

4. important new knowledge and theory of science as well as their functioning as direct productive forces in socialist society.

The primary objective of the curricula modification program was that of making qualitative changes for the purpose of improving possiblities and foundations for the overall development of socialist personalities. As a consequence of this objective:

new subjects were included in the curricula and antiquated ones sorted out; the newly chosen curricula were rearranged, accentuated, given an appropriate structure and suitably coordinated. . . . At the same time opinion about the nature of teaching subjects underwent a change. Way and manner to acquire knowledge, abilities, skills, the formation of conduct, consciousness and character were integrated into the conception of the "subject" (des "Stoffes") and more fully taken into account. Starting from the law that it is aim that determines contents but both [aim and contents] together [that determine] the process of education and training, the curricula at the same time represent a new didactic conception. . . . This didactic conception is a well-balanced synthesis both of proved and fresh elements in the sense of a diversified teaching and learning. Goals and partial goals of lessons for example are more accurately planned, the courses largely coordinated among each other and the didactic process during lessons proper more precisely preplanned in its complexity.[7]

The resultant curricula, which form the basis of contemporary mandatory education in the GDR, were introduced into the educational program of the ten-year general polytechnical secondary school according to the following schedule: into the first grade in 1965, the second and fifth grades in 1966, the third and sixth grades in 1967, the fourth and seventh grades in 1968, into the ninth grade in 1970, and the tenth grade in 1971.

The curricula are kept current by various means; particularly, by suggestions emanating from the local level, such as from subject-specific advisors and from the teachers themselves. The fifteen regional districts, or *Bezirke*, into which the GDR is divided, are further sub-divided into 219 city and rural local districts, or *Kreise*. Each of the 219 *Kreise* has advisors for schools within the *Kreis* who devote a certain amount of time each week to carrying out various investiga-tions related to assessing the stability of the curricula. On the basis of these investigations, it has been determined that the science curri-cula, for example, are valid and will retain their validity into the near future.[8]

The stability of the curricula in all areas of instruction in the ten-year general polytechnical secondary schools are considered by GDR pedagogical scientists to be of the greatest importance. The curricula are the basis of education in these schools and, therefore, the effective-ness and stability of the entire system of East German compulsory education is dependent on their stability and versatility.[9]

A discussion of teaching methods used in the ten-year general polytechnical secondary schools must be preceded with a considera-tion of how the instructional process, as it is perceived by pedagogi-cal scientists in the GDR, relates to the epistemology of dialectical materialism.

According to the Marxist-Leninist point of view, in the process of physical and intellectual development, the individual evolves an in-ternal model of the external (natural and social) environment. Inter-action with the environment is based upon the level of development of this internal model: the individual's interactions with the natural and social environment will be successful to the extent that his or her internal model correctly reflects external reality. In this sense, the process of acquiring knowledge is viewed predominantly as a process of developing the individual's internal model of the external world so that his internal model approximates external reality with ever increasing accuracy. In socialist society, teaching is perceived as the setting of objectives and the management of this process of ap-proximation. Education, therefore, is basically the process of align-ing the individual's internal model of reality with the Marxist-Leninist concept of the external world.[10]

The Marxist-Leninist approach to the education and training of children is based on recognition of the inequality, or variation, of in-dividual abilities. According to Marx, individuals "would not be dif-ferent individuals if they were not unequal."[11] Marxism-Leninism teaches that human abilities develop and form through the process of activity; and, the variation of human abilities is manifest in human activity. Human ability, therefore, must be judged by its results in activity.[12]

Individual differences in ability are considered by Marxist-Lenin-ists to be the result of biological and social factors:

> Natural gifts are only conditions for the development of abilities; their actual development takes place in the course of the life of the in-dividual under the influence of training, education and self-education, in the course of his work and social activity. The character of an indivi-dual's abilities is also influenced by the general conditions of social life and the immediate social environment (family, neighbours, workmates, acquaintances, etc.), that is, the micro-environment, which also includes various accidental factors that sometimes cannot be taken into account.

> What then are the conditions of the social environment that encour-age the formation and development of abilities? To this question Marx and Engels gave the following answer: 'Only in community (with others) has each individual the means of cultivating his gifts in all directions; only in the community, therefore, is personal freedom possible.'[13]

The development of human abilities, however, depends upon the in-dividual's will to achieve certain goals:

> Like other abilities, will power is also not merely a gift of nature; it is born and tempered in activity. No matter how significant personal in-centives in the form of personal material interest or the spiritual satis-faction obtained from social praise, it is the spirit of solidarity and mu-tual dedication developed in the course of collective work that fosters will power and thus multiplies the energy and abilities of the individual.

> . . . By its very nature a collective is an arena for the expression and development of individual energies and abilities, for individual freedom.[14]

In Marxist-Leninist terminology, a collective is composed of a group of individuals who sublimate their egotism for the purpose of promoting the welfare of the group. Within the framework of social-ist society, the individual is first considered to be a member of a col-lective:

> Under socialism society forms an integrated *collective entity*. All the groups of which it is composed—social communities, work collectives, various kinds of associations—are bound together by the community of their interests, which is rooted in the material needs of the whole of society.[15]

In this context, human abilities are judged positively when the result-ant related activity contributes to the common welfare.

Collectives function on the principle of mutual assistance and, ac-cording to Marxist-Leninist theoreticians, working and learning in a collective environment "helps the individual to activate his potential, to stimulate his energies and abilities."[16] In keeping with this posi-tion, the primary milieu in which the process of education and train-ing occurs in the GDR general schools is that of the learning collec-tive—a class of approximately thirty children of nearly the same age.

The learning collective is an environment in which the teaching and learning of subject matter is combined with the development of socialist morality. Accordingly, the learning collective is guided by the following major principles of socialist character education:[17]

1. The peer [learning] collective (under adult leadership) rivals and early surpasses the family as the principal agent of socialization.

2. Competition between groups is utilized as the principal mechanism for motivating achievement of behavior norms.

3. The behavior of the individual is evaluated primarily in terms of its relevance to the goals and achievements of the collective.

4. Rewards and punishments are frequently given on a group basis; that is to say, the entire group benefits or suffers as a consequence of the conduct of individual members.

5. As soon as possible, the tasks of evaluating the behavior of individuals and of dispensing rewards and sanctions is delegated to the members of the collective.

6. The principal methods of social control are public recognition and public criticism, with explicit training and practice being given in these activities. Specifically, each member of the collective is encouraged to observe deviant behavior by his fellows and is given opportunity to report his observations to the group. Reporting on one's peers is esteemed and rewarded as a civic duty.

7. Group criticism becomes the vehicle for training in self-criticism in the presence of one's peers. Such public self-criticism is regarded as a powerful mechanism for maintaining and enhancing commitment to approved standards of behavior, as well as the method of choice for bringing deviants back into line.

Pedagogical scientists in the GDR and in other socialist countries consider the process of learning in a collective environment to be an essential experience for the nation's youth for the purpose of ensuring their future effective participation in the industrial and agricultural collectives of socialist industry.

Superficially, the teaching methods used in the ten-year general polytechnical secondary school in the GDR and the physical setting of the school environment are familiar. The basic organizational form is the class composed of approximately thirty children (somewhat less in higher grades) of nearly the same age. An instructional period is forty-five minutes in length and is composed of a series of instructional units, the length and characterization of which depend on the topic under consideration as well as on the instructional goals.[18] The definitive foundation of education and training in the GDR general schools is the subject and grade level differentiated curriculum which includes the instructional goals and contents of the subject and determines the outline of the pedagogical process.[19]

In the ten-year general polytechnical secondary school, instruction is based upon the "dialectical unity of the acquisition of knowledge, the development of abilities, and socialist training" and:

it proceeds according to the principles of the Marxist-Leninist theory of knowledge and the laws of dialectics which prove that the educational process is the essential foundation for the personality development of the student.[20]

During the Seventh Pedagogical Congress of the GDR, which met between May 5 and 7, 1970, in Berlin, it was emphasized that no distinction was to be made between traditional methods and new teaching methods in the instructional process; but, rather, that contemporary education should be a harmonious blend of the traditional and the new:

> At the congress discussion, it was confirmed that one must continually examine whether this or that method in this subject, in this grade, in this or that instructional unit is, at any given time, the most favorable manner of realizing the instructional goals, that one must fully utilize the abundant wealth of knowledge of didactic methodology and proven methods and [that one] must strive to develop new methods.[21]

The tasks of fulfilling educational objectives as well as of developing the talents and skills of the students are considered to be dependent upon the creative application of the total knowledge of teaching methodology:

> It is essential that the numerous instructional methods and forms of instructional organization are properly utilized and that, at any given time, the most effective methods are chosen with regard to the concrete situation in the [classroom] as well as to the developmental level of the individual students. Accordingly, experienced teachers determine the differentiated measures that are necessary in [specific] sections of the instructional process. They are continually guided by [the concept] that the powers of the collective must be employed for the development of the individual capabilities of each student.
>
> An active, versatile instruction which concentrates on the essential, on the conscious development and guidance of the independent activity of the students is promoted by the application of such established principles as practice, consolidation and repetition, observation and comprehension, as well as by a problem-rich presentation of the teaching material, work with differentiated problem situations, the utilization of work-oriented experiences and the correct didactic insertion of instructional aids.[22]

This statement by the minister of education of the GDR, Margot Honecker, is a synopsis of what is presently regarded as being the most effective approach to teaching at the level of compulsory education in the GDR.

Within the sphere of socialist education, the learning process is considered to be "a unified process of acquisition of knowledge, skills, and behavioral qualities by the student and the development of the total personality under the leadership of the teacher," and instructional methods are described as a "general process by which, with consideration of concrete goals, contents, and conditions, one can attain instructional success with great certainty."[23]

The primary form for organizing instruction is the instructional period. It is constructed of instructional units with specific goals. In general, instructional units are selected for their contribution towards achieving the major instructional goal of the period. According to GDR educators, the general requirements for a successful instructional period are:[24]

    1. an interesting, relevant, goal-oriented, problem-rich formulation of instruction that is directed towards the subject matter to be mastered;

    2. systematic consolidation, exercise, review, and systematization as non-negotiable prerequisites for secure and permanent knowledge and understanding;

    3. versatile application of what has been learned; [and]

    4. continual checking of knowledge and understanding is particularly important for intensive learning and effective training.

The methodological construction of the instructional period is based on the teacher's understanding of the goals of instruction, the subject matter to be taught, and the pertinent curriculum. The choice of teaching methods and their combination should be based on the potential they have for the individual student and the learning collective with regard to "personality development, the acquisition of knowledge and understanding, the further development of capabilities and skills, and the consolidation of socialist character qualities, habits, attitudes, and conviction."[25]

According to pedagogical scientists in the GDR, the fundamental difference between instructional methods used in socialist education and those employed in the traditional democracies of the West is that socialist methods of instruction include the guiding activity of the teacher with regard to the logical development of subject matter as well as the teacher's socialist conviction and ability for successful interaction with the learning collective.[26]

Instructional methods are classified on the basis of the type and manner of teacher-student interaction. The three basic methods of instruction are (1) the method of presentation, (2) the method of collective work, and (3) the method of independent work.

The major forms of the instructional method of presentation are the teacher-lecture, the student-lecture, and the demonstration. During the teacher-lecture, the teacher presents essential components of the subject matter primarily through use of the potentialities of speech—by informing, reporting, relating, describing, and explaining—

PLATES

I.   *The period in which grandfather lived comes alive when the history of events at the turn of the century are taught by a specialist teacher in History and German at the Judith Auer Ten-Year General Polytechnical Secondary School in the Koepenick section of Berlin. (June 11, 1976.)*

II. *The Otto Grotewohl Ten-Year General Polytechnical Secondary School in the Pankow section of Berlin. Girls and boys carry out the work of tending a school garden under the direction of a primary grade teacher. Students acquire practical knowledge through the subject "School Garden Instruction" in the primary stage of compulsory education. (May 7, 1974.)*

III. *A laboratory, or* Praktikum, *in creative sculpture for students from Neustrelitz, District of Neubrandenburg. The traditional student* Praktikum *in art instruction was held for the ninth time in the Jawaharlal Nehru Ten-Year General Polytechnical Secondary School in Neustrelitz. More than 90 students participated in acquiring the fundamentals of sculpting under the direction of art instructors. (February 15, 1977.)*

IV. *Approximately 1800 girls and boys acquire first-hand work experience in socialist production once each week in the Polytechnical Centrum of the Frankfurt Semi-Conductor Works, Frankfurt on the Oder. (November 9, 1978.)*

V.   *An eighth grade class during an instruction period in the special instruction room for geography at the Otto Grotewohl Ten-Year General Secondary School, District Suhl. This is one of the two schools recently built in the newly constructed area in Illmenau, and is attended by 850 students. 250,000 marks were spent to provide 26 classrooms and 15 special instruction rooms for the use of these young people. (April 11, 1978.)*

VI. *Young "artists" eagerly at work. The theme of this instruction period in drawing for fifth graders of the Thomas Muenzer Ten-Year General Polytechnical Secondary School in Sangerhausen (Halle) is: "We Promote Sports." (July 2, 1974.)*

PLATES

VII. *Eighth graders from the school in Dedelow, a village of socialist agriculture. "Productive Work" is an aspect of their education. All students of this age, whether they live in the city or in the countryside, are required to complete this type of course. Boys and girls who live in the cities do their "Productive Work" in industrial enterprises. In Dedelow, the productive work of the students involves learning the fundamentals of plant and animal production. Here the students are shown planting cabbages in fields that belong to the* Landwirtschaftlich Produktionsgenossenschaft *(LPG), an agricultural production cooperative. (September, 1974.)*

VIII. *A fourth grade class receives music instruction in the new Thomas Extended General Polytechnical Secondary School in Leipzig, the training place of the world famous* Thomaner *singers, where 490 students recently began classes. As an exception, students begin attending this school in the fourth grade so that they can fulfill the requirements for compulsory education while at the same time training and meeting the demands imposed by continual concert tours. (April 11, 1973.)*

IX. *Work instruction in the Ten-Year General Polytechnical Seccondary School No. 52, in Dresden. Sixth graders are shown here doing productive work. They are making a part that will later be used by construction workers. (June 22, 1972.)*

X. *The Ernst Thaelmann Ten-Year General Polytechnical Secondary School in Mueringsdorf (southeast Weimar) has been expanded with a new building. In September 1970 at the beginning of the snew school year, new modern classrooms were available in this section of the building. (February 24, 1975.)*

XI. *A typical modernly-equipped biology-chemistry lab in the new village specialized school in Knau. With an investment of 3.5 million marks and 22,000 hours volunteered by teachers, pupils, and parents, it was built within one year. School busses bring 300 students and 10 staff members from the Oberland Cooperative to this modern building. (October 8, 1977.)*

PLATES

XII.   *Instruction for 700 students began in the new school build-*
       ing at Mueritz-Stadt Roebel in Neubrandenburg in Roebel
       at the beginning of May. In addition to 26 classrooms, there
       are a large number of special instruction rooms. Here, in the
       chemistry room, seventh graders Rainer Zache and Chris-
       tine Jarchow are making oxygen under the direction of the
       specialized teacher Antje Gromodka. (March 23, 1972.)

XIII. *Physics instruction in the ninth grade of the Ten-Year Gen-*
       eral Polytechnical Secondary School in Berlstedt. This is one
       of the special instruction rooms in the school. There are also
       chemistry and biology labs in which every student can per-
       form practical experiments from his own desk. The Poly-
       technical Secondary School in Berlstedt is attended by 723
       students from 12 surrounding localities.

ADN Photographs Supplied by the GDR Ministry of Education

Plate I.

Plate II.

Plate III.

Plate IV.

Plate V.

Plate VI.

Plate VII.

Plate VIII.

Plate IX.

Plate X.

Plate XI.

Plate XII.

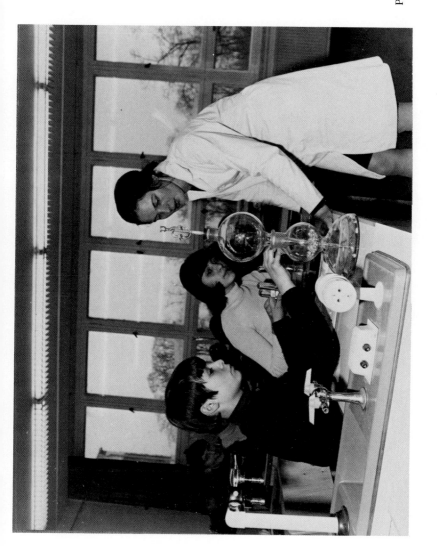

Plate XIII.

and combines it with instructional aids and organizes systematic listening, participatory thinking, and intellectual treatment of the subject matter including various processes of consolidation. The length of the teacher-lecture depends, to a great extent, on the developmental level of the students and also on the subject matter under consideration. An objective of this instructional form is to develop the students' ability to understand oral presentations.[27]

The requirements of the student-lecture are essentially the same as for the teacher-lecture. Goals are: (1) to enrich instruction through the variation of instructional form; (2) to give students experience in the oral presentation of a topic; and (3) to assist and promote the development of weaker students by encouraging the growth of their self-confidence.[28]

Demonstration includes showing objects, phenomena, and processes with the assistance of instructional aids or directly from nature. It also includes showing activities and modes of behavior. In this form of presentation, the medium of speech is secondary to the demonstration, but retains its importance as a means of clarification. The instructional success of a demonstration depends on the teacher's ability to bring about a unity of sensory perception and intellectual processing, active observation and abstract thought. Attainment of this unity is largely the result of a meaningful combination of the teacher's explanation with events that transpire during the course of the demonstration. While the demonstration is taking place, student activities, such as participatory thinking and intellectual treatment, are combined with experiences such as taking notes, illustrating, and providing commentary.[29]

Use of the method of collective work is recommended when preliminary student knowledge in the form of information and experiences can be assumed by the teacher and used as a basis for further topic development through the effort of the collective. Two forms of this method of instruction are the *Unterrichtsgespraech* (instructional conversation or colloquy) and the classroom discussion.

An instructional colloquy is a didactically developed conversation guided by the teacher. Through the process of asking questions and posing problems, the teacher stimulates the course and direction of student thought and thus guides the students towards understanding. The objectives of this form of instruction are:

> to motivate students to independent thought which enables them to search for hypotheses and methods of solution, promotes [the desire] to substantiate and prove, develops their ability to debate, and makes the potential of the collective available for the individualized process of acquiring knowledge and forming [political] conviction.[31]

Classroom discussion is characterized by the corroboration, or substantiation, of different points of view and interpretations. The objective of this form of collective work is to develop a critical attitude in the students. The major difference between the instructional colloquy and the classroom discussion is that the latter requires a greater degree of student independence: the teacher intercedes only when the discussion is stalled or digressed. Prerequisites for a genuine classroom discussion are questions, problems, or topics that have student relevance and with which they are intellectually occupied.

According to Marxist-Leninist pedagogical scientists and psychologists, people are not only objects to be influenced by the environment, but they are also active subjects who have within themselves the ability to change the environment. This concept is the basis of independent student activity in the GDR general schools. Activity, it is recalled, is the expression of individual ability and it is on the basis of activity that abilities are judged. Accordingly, a significant role is ascribed to activity:

> Activity must be an aspect of the total personality of the young person and must activate, not only this or that side [of the personality], but rather the essence of his being so that he naturally concentrates on the task put before him.[32]

Two of the most common forms of independent student activity are student experiments which are integrated into the process of science instruction and textbook work. Their major pedagogical significance is to be found in the independent acquisition of knowledge and understanding by students through their own practical intellectual activity. GDR educators contend that the experiments done by students in science classes should be both a source of pleasure and interest motivation.

Student experiments are carried out in a laboratory or in a specially equipped course instruction room called a *Fachunterrichtszimmer* which contains appropriate equipment. The teacher organizes the student experiement and directs, assists, and supervises the experimental activity; the students work independently or in groups. Student activity generally involves setting up and testing hypotheses or formulating questions; solving the practical problems of experimental procedure; observing and recording experimental results; and evaluating various experimental procedures on the basis of practice. A major objective of this form of independent student activity is to develop skills and personality characteristics—goal orientation, concentration, exactness, order, will-power, and the desire to experiment—

that are viewed as essential for future effective work in socialist agricultural and industrial collectives.[33]

The independent student activity of working with textbooks of various kinds is an instructional form used for acquiring knowledge. Student activity is guided by the teacher for the purpose of organizing required learning activities, establishing proper procedures for working with books, as well as supplementing, explaining, aiding, and checking student book work.[34] Other forms of independent student activity that are teacher-guided are observing and learning by inquiry, practical activity, and the solution of learning and problem exercises.

The basic teaching methods—presentation, collective work, and independent student activity—are related to learning processes on the basis of the instructional function that is to be fulfilled. Successful attainment of learning objectives is viewed as a consequence of the teacher's creative use of various teaching methods for the purpose of evoking desirable student learning processes within the context of a given instructional function.

Desirable learning methods have been classified by pedagogical scientists in the GDR under headings that are descriptive of the intended student response: receptive, reproductive, applicative, and productive. Two receptive, but not passive, learning forms are: absorbing and processing what is heard and observing and processing what is seen. Reproductive forms of learning are reproduction in oral and written form and experimental work. Applicative forms are identified as the solution of exercises and experimental work, and productive forms of learning involve the solution of exercises that promote discovery of unknown relationships and experimental work.[35]

The major instructional functions to be accomplished as a result of eliciting these learning methods are (1) the introduction and processing of new subject matter, (2) the consolidation of subject matter, and (3) checking and evaluating teaching and learning objectives.

During the introduction of new subject matter,[36] the three major tasks to be fulfilled are (1) review and verification of previously learned, relevant material; (2) provision of information and concepts that are essential for processing the new topic; and, (3) stimulation of student interest and attention. The level of approach to a new topic is established largely through review. In this manner, students are made aware of the knowledge and understandings considered to be basic for an adquate comprehension of the new subject matter. According to GDR educators, interest and curiosity in a new topic should be elicited through social motivation, that is, by relating the topic to contemporary problems so that students become conscious of its social or economic significance.

Pedagogical scientists in the socialist countries consider teaching and learning to be most effective when they are guided by goals. Students should be informed of the major goal of the instructional period as well as of individual goals of the instructional sections that comprise the period. Goal orientation towards new material should be accompanied by motivation. For example, in the case of chemistry instruction the following approach is recommended for setting goals in preparation for teaching a process by which ammonia is manufactured in GDR industry:

> During the [1970-75] Five Year Plan, approximately one-half of the increase in the production of the plants [was] to be achieved by chemical means, predominantly, through the application of fertilizers and prophylactic treatment. Between 1970 and 1975, the requirements of the Eighth Party Congress [were] that the preparation of fertilizer obtained from nitrogen [was to] be increased from 529,000 to 800,000 tons. Nitrogen fertilizer is fed to the soil, in part, in the form of ammonia.... Today we will learn about a technical process by which ammonia is produced.[37]

Motivational materials should be relatively current and topical issues and examples are preferred for developing student interest and curiosity in new topics. The method of introducing and processing new subject matter depends on instructional goals, the developmental level of the students, and on the subject matter itself.

The purpose of consolidation is to inform students of the learning objectives associated with new subject matter so that they will be able to apply the theoretical and practical information that they will acquire on an operational level:

> The major learning objective, including all its partial aspects, and the associated motivations, elements of conviction, political viewpoints, and other personality characteristics must be unequivocally and recognizably crystallized for all students and grasped by them.[38]

Major forms of consolidation are review, application, practice or exercise, and systematization. Review involves the repeated performance of an intellectual or practical activity by the teacher or student. Application is defined as a "relatively independent and creative operation" in which the acquired knowledge and understandings are applied under "new conditions" and in "new situations and relationships." Practice, or exercise, is the repeated performance of activities with the goal of perfecting them into skills and habits.[39]

In general, the major teaching methods—presentation, collective work, and independent work—are all evoked for the instructional function of consolidation. A primary difference between independent student activity as it is related to working on new subject matter and to consolidation is that in the latter case the range of independent work is greater. For example, exercises assigned for the purpose of consolidation include material that the students have not yet mastered so that they can apply their knowledge towards making new discoveries.

The checking and evaluation of teaching effectiveness is considered to be an essential aspect of instruction by East German educators. The teacher should continually gather information concerning the progress and results of instruction so that erroneous developments can be recognized early and corrected. Student performance must be evaluated so that students can be made aware of their development and progress. The contention is that this information contributes to the development of self-confidence and a critical attitude towards achievement on the part of the students.[40]

Continual checking of the learning process and its results is often closely associated with other instructional functions. For example, a teacher gains important information concerning the level of attainment of learning objective through observing student collaboration during the instructional functions of working with new subject matter and consolidation, manifestations of student confidence in the solution of assigned exercises and problems, and overall student behavior. In general, the manner in which student progress is checked and evaluated is considered by GDR educators to be the major determining factor in the teacher-student relationship. They contend that characteristics such as honesty, confidence in the teacher and in the collective, self-critical behavior, and responsibility are all promoted in students when the teacher-student relationship is a positive one.[41]

Although much emphasis is placed on independent student activity in GDR compulsory schools, individualized programmed learning is not generally employed in the instructional process. Research concerning the utilization and effectiveness of programmed learning is currently in progress in the GDR in cooperation with the Soviet Union.

The Academy of Pedagogical Sciences of the GDR recently completed a major research project in which fifteen programmed learning plans that had been developed by teachers, methodologists, and science specialists were tested. One hundred and sixty school classes, composed of approximately 5,000 students, participated in the experiment which resulted in the calculation of 1,000 correlation coefficients.[42]

Analysis of the experimental results yielded information concerning both the possibilities and limitations of programmed learning and teaching. It was demonstrated that programmed teaching and learning was not an alternative to traditional methods of teaching. The experiment showed that essential personality qualities such as the ability of constructive collaboration and creative formulation of dialectic and perspicacious thought as well as the capacity to solve exercises on the basis of effective statements could not be adequately developed through the use of programmed materials and learning machines. Attainment of these qualities is clearly determined by the leading voice of the teacher and his or her creative pedagogical work.[43] In conjunction with these conclusions, at the Seventh Pedagogical Congress it was stated that:

> the various bourgeois learning theories upon which programmed instruction is based in the capitalist countries essentially reduce the learning process to an incentive-reaction-scheme and individualized learning processes that are too dispersed and largely independent of each other. They contradict our Marxist-Leninist concept of instruction as a creative process in which the individual and the collective advance reciprocally and in which all aspects of the person are developed. They are, therefore, unacceptable for [use] in the socialist school.[44]

Utilization of programmed learning techniques for instructional purposes in the ten-year general polytechnical secondary school is generally confined to catering specific student interests on an extracurricular basis.[45]

A basic tenet of GDR educators is that all children and young people who attend the ten-year general polytechnical secondary school are capable of learning the subject matter presented in all of the courses of study.[46] It is recognized, however, that students will demonstrate varying levels of learning comprehension and scholastic achievement within a given learning collective. According to pedagogical scientists in the GDR, there is a direct relation between student achievement and student motivation. Motivation is considered to be dependent on environmental factors. In this regard, particular stress is placed on a home environment in which learning is esteemed. Students whose scholastic achievement is inadequate are considered as coming from defective home environments.

Efforts are made to correct the detrimental effects of defective home environments on pupils' scholastic achievement through relationships known as the *Patenschaft*, through teacher-parent consultations, and through interaction of the *Eltern Aktiven*, or parents' councils, with the parents of students whose achievement is inadequate.

One form of the *Patenschaft* is a student-to-student relationship in which a high-achieving student offers assistance for learning to a low-achieving student. An obvious purpose of this relationship is to correct a defect in the learning environment of the low-achieving student, or to compensate for an inadequate home environment, through increased attention and remedial work. It is contended that this kind of additional attention and work will result in increasing the low-achiever's motivation and scholastic achievement.

The less obvious purpose of this form of *Patenschaft* is the training that it provides in "anti-egotism" for the high-achieving student. Young people, it is maintained, must learn to consider their abilities in terms of services that can be rendered to socialist society in the GDR. Achievement of individual students is significant only in the sense that it enhances or undermines the collective achievement, and students are responsible for utilizing their scholastic achievement for the benefit of the collective. The *Patenschaft* relationship is considered to be a form of training in social obligation.

At the Eighth Educational Congress of the GDR, held in Berlin during October 18-20, 1978, the minister of education, Margot Honecker, made the following comments regarding methods of teaching in the compulsory schools:

> Much of the debate [at the congress] has revolved around methods of teaching because, to a large extent, they determine whether the knowledge and skills taught at school are of lasting value and easy to apply in practice and whether pupils are encouraged to use their powers of reasoning, whether teachers appeal to their finer feelings and achieve their educational purpose. We know that if the quality of the subject matter taught falls short of requirements, this cannot be offset by a good general approach to classroom work. Conversely, if teaching methods prove inadquate, this cannot be made up for by the content of specialist education. Many of our colleagues have pointed out that as far as methodology is concerned, rigid systems are as undesirable as routine and formalism which creep all too easily into our daily work. Every member of our profession knows full well that there is a constant need to revise and experiment so as to find out which methods will lead to the best results in a given subject or class.[47]

The general approach to the further development of teaching methodology in the area of compulsory education is that recommendations initiated on the local level by teachers are submitted in written form to higher authorities in the field of pedagogical science. Recommendations that withstand examination and testing at the level of the Academy of Pedagogical Sciences are subsequently implemented at the national level.

Teacher conferences in specific subject areas are held every two years allowing for the exchange of ideas and experiences for the purpose of improving teaching and learning effectiveness. These conferences are held at the national level and also at the international level among the socialist countries of Eastern Europe. Written reports submitted in conjunction with these conferences are published in the appropriate journals and thus become available for further consideration. Reports from conferences held at the national level as well as individual articles written by teachers and methodologists are published in teaching journals devoted to specific subject specialties. For example, the journal *Physik in der Schule*, or "Physics in the School," is a monthly publication and the medium through which physics teachers can make recommendations for improving the methodology of physics teaching.

Efforts are continually made to consider increasingly more detailed aspects of contemporary teaching methods to aid teachers in maximizing student learning effectiveness. However, at the Eighth Educational Congress, teachers were reminded that "practice has shown that the results achieved depend largely on the quality of each lesson and the preparations that go into it, a matter which no teacher, whether he is young or very experienced, must underestimate."[48]

Since the skill with which a teacher is able to develop interesting and effective lessons depends, to a great extent, on the way in which the teacher is trained and educated, we will next turn to a consideration of the professional training required of teachers in the GDR.

CHAPTER VI

TEACHERS

At the Eighth Educational Congress, the minister of education of the GDR stressed that:

> The teacher in present-day society is facing an exacting task in that he is now bringing up that generation which in the prime of its life will complete socialism and carry out the transition to communism. . . .
>
> The teaching profession requires personal commitment, love of children, a strong sense of duty. The successful outcome of education in the spirit of communism in great measure depends on the teacher's ideological stance, his political and moral conviction and attitude, scientific education, cultural level, and on his personality.[1]

Examining the way in which teachers are trained in the GDR to develop these proficiencies, let us first take a look at the legal bases for the professional education of teachers for the ten-year general polytechnical secondary school. According to the Act on the Integrated Socialist Educational System:

> (1) The implementation of the integrated socialist educational system necessitates the training of patriotic and scientifically qualified teachers and educators in sufficient numbers. This training takes place at universities, colleges, institutes of education, teacher training institutes, and pedagogical schools for kindergarten teachers.
>
> (2) The Minister of Education determines the principles for the training of teachers and educators, and confirms the curricula. The State Secretariat for Higher and Technical Education and the other central government and economic authorities, in whose fields of competence teachers are trained, are responsible for the practical application of these principles and for the content of the training on the basis of the curricula in the institutions subordinate to them. . . .
>
> (3) The science of Marxism-Leninism shall be imparted to the students in connection with practical life.
>
> (4) The training in pedagogics, psychology, and methodology shall be distinguished by a high theoretical level. The sections of the practical training carried through in the schools are of special importance. Close interrelations shall be established between practical work at school and the course of studies. In the process of training the findings of science shall be connected with the experiences of the innovators in education.[2]

Thus, teachers for the ten-year general and extended polytechnical secondary schools are educated and trained in universities, colleges, and pedagogical institutes according to a compulsory curriculum which has been confirmed by the minister of education. The principles that form the basis for this curriculum are furnished by the philosophy of historical and dialectical materialism, and, the practical application of theoretical knowledge is emphasized.

Teachers for the ten-year general polytechnical secondary school are trained according to two programs, depending on whether they intend to become qualified for teaching grades 1 through 4 or grades 5 through 12.

The training of teachers for the first four grades is based on a four year program undertaken in teacher training institutes. Students are qualified to begin this program upon completion of the ten-year period of compulsory education. The training emphasis is on educational theory as it relates to the developmental progress of early childhood and on the German language and mathematics. Graduates of the teacher training institutes are qualified to teach three subjects in grades 1 through 4—German, mathematics, and one of the following: music, physical education, art education, manual training, or gardening.[3]

Teachers for grades 5 through 12 are trained and educated on the basis of programs that depend on their major and minor fields of specialization. Contrary to what is often the case in the West, young people who prepare for careers as teachers of grades 5 through 12 in the GDR must be in the upper 10 percent of their compulsory school class in order to qualify for university preparation in the eleventh and twelfth grades. Thus, intermediate and secondary stage teachers in GDR compulsory schools are among the brightest of their peers. Their training is delineated in general terms as follows:[4]

1. Future teachers are educated and trained in the departments of universities that correspond to their teaching specialty or in pedagogical universities according to the same learning program.

2. The prerequisites for entry into the education and training program are the successful attainment of the *Abitur* and the planned, future availability of teaching positions in the various areas of academic instruction.

3. The period of education and training is four years.

4. Secondary-level general school teacher aspirants are trained to teach two subjects; thus, they have a major subject emphasis and a minor subject emphasis. (Teacher aspirants who are being trained to

teach polytechnical subjects in the general schools have a one-subject emphasis, i.e., polytechnical education, since teacher training in this area involves a wide range of disciplines. Physical education and music teachers can be trained in special institutes without the requirement of a two-subject specialty teaching combination.)

5. Teachers graduating from the secondary-level general school teacher training program are qualified to teach the two subjects in which they specialized at all levels of the ten-year general and extended polytechnical secondary schools.

The education and training of teachers of grades 5 through 12 is comprised of two stages, each of which involves two years of study. The major function of the first two-year period is to provide "a broad, fundamental scientific training" in the disciplines of the teacher aspirant's specialty combination. The second two-year period is characterized by increased specialization in the major subject with an emphasis on individual work for purposes of acquiring knowledge and applying this knowledge to professional problems.[5]

The basic courses of the first stage of teacher training are devoted to "general theoretical and methodological fundamentals of the various subjects and the educational sciences."[6] All students, regardless of the training institution or the combination of specialty subjects, study the following disciplines during the first two years: Marxism-Leninism, pedagogy, psychology, political-pedagogical activity, an introduction to the methodology of teaching in the major and minor fields of specialization, the Russian language, sports, speech training, the techniques of working with audio-visual instructional aids, cultural-aesthetic education and training, and fundamental courses in the major and minor fields.

Areas of study during the second stage of teacher training include continued study in the major and minor fields with an emphasis on the major field of specialization, extensive work in the teaching methodology of the major field, and student sports as well as further study, with decreased emphasis, in Marxism-Leninism, pedagogy, and psychology. (Table 6-1). Work done in the elective course generally leads to the theme of a thesis that must be submitted by the teacher aspirant in partial fulfillment of the requirements for qualification as a specialist teacher.[8]

Education and training in pedagogy and psychology extends over the entire four-year period of teacher training. The primary objective of study in this area is to enable future specialist teachers to:

TABLE 6-1[7]

Schedule of Courses Required for Teacher Qualification

Course	Hours of Study Required				Semester*							
	Total	Lecture	Seminar	Lab	1	2	3	4	5	6	7	8
Marxism-Leninism	299	149	150		3	2	4	4	3	3	1	
Pedagogy	134	75	59		2	2	2	2		1		
Psychology	116	44	72		2	2	2	2			2	
Political-Pedagogical Activity	64		32	32	2							
Methodology of the Major and Minor Fields of Specialization	250							2	6	4	4	
Russian Language	76		76		2	2	1					
Student Sports	212				2	2	2	2	2	2	2	
Speech Training	12		12				1					
Techniques of Working with Audio-Visual Instructional Aids	16	6	10			1						
Cultural-Aesthetic Education and Training	32		32		1	1						
Elective Course	189								4	5	3	
Major Field of Specialization	1090[†]	(Cf. below, Table 6-2)										
Minor Field of Specialization	690[†]	(Cf. below, Table 6-2)										

* Numbers equal hours of instruction per week.

† Represents an average figure; slight variation in total hours required depending on fields of specialization.

scientifically solve, in theory and practice, all the pedagogical and psychological problems arising with respect to the individual child's personality and the collective behavior of classes, so that the educational policy pursued by [GDR] society can be carried through and the objectives of [the curricula] can be attained to the optimum by creative classroom work. Studies are related to practical work and must bring about the skills required to efficiently conduct the educational processes.[9]

The first year of education and training in pedagogy and psychology consists of a fundamental course which includes a study of teenage psychology and the psychological problems related to that period of human development, the problems of socialist education and training, and selected problems related to teaching at the secondary level. The second-year course in pedagogy and psychology includes work in socialist educational theory and dialectics. Objectives of this course are to develop:

the abilities, skills and convictions that are required for the [teacher aspirants] to understand the significance of teaching in the overall system of education, grasp the scientific character of teaching and do successful classroom work.[10]

The second year course is also intended to educate future specialist teachers in the following three principles by which they are to be guided as professionals:[11]

1. Classroom teaching and learning is the major element of education and is to be organized in view of latest know-how in socialist pedagogics.

2. The [curricula] applied in the general polytechnical secondary school are the basis of the work to be done. Efficient teaching and learning are first of all defined by the objectives laid down in the [curricula].

3. Classroom work in [GDR] schools is to be considered a development of the progressive heritage in didactics and a result of generalizing experiences gained with the educational systems of the other socialist countries.

Additionally, second-year studies in pedagogy and psychology include topics in individual and collective psychological diagnosis for the purpose of teaching future specialist teachers to:

apply the laws, theories, and terms of psychology (such as the theory of learning, the theory of abilities) on their own, recognize their [effect] on individuals and groups and draw conclusions for their own work leading to changes in practice.[12]

The fundamental introductory courses in pedagogy and psychology are studied during the first two years of teacher training. During the last half of the fourth year, a final mandatory course in educational science has as its objective the integration of pedagogy, psychology, and the methodology of teaching. In addition, students are familiarized with "topical problems of long-term educational policy and with the latest findings of research work in pedagogics and psychology."[13]

The subject area entitled "Fundamentals of Marxism-Leninism" is comprised of three courses: (1) dialectical and historical materialism, (2) political economy of capitalism and socialism, and (3) scientific communism: fundamental lessons drawn from the history of the working-class movement.[14]

Objectives of the study of Marxism-Leninism in these courses are:

1. [to aid in the training of] highly qualified personalities, mature in terms of morals and character, who have a consolidated scientific ideology and are capable of dialectic thought, [and]

2. to convince [teacher aspirants] that Marxism-Leninism is the *only* scientific philosophy and provides the basis for solving theoretical and practical problems of our days [*italics not in the original*].[15]

Education and training in the major and minor subject areas is characterized by a first two-year stage during which time the students acquire a fundamental knowledge in both subject areas for the purpose of ensuring future "scientific teaching" of the subject in the general and extended secondary schools. The second two-year stage of specialty training features further work in the major subject area, which continues with increased intensity, and the virtual termination of training in the minor subject area.[16]

Education and training in the major subject area must meet the following requirements:[17]

1. It [must ensure] that the future specialist teachers receive a thorough grounding in principal relations and laws as well as the specific ways of thinking and working in the sphere of science involved.

2. [It must ensure that the specialized teachers will acquire] a general knowledge of the major research problems and trends in the scientific field [in which] they are going to teach.

3. [The specialist teachers] must be able to correctly evaluate [the major subject area's] function within the framework of the uniform socialist system of education.

These requirements are met primarily in the elective course which is designed to provide the opportunity for students to become scientifically involved in their major field of specialty.

The period of fundamental education and training in the major and minor subject areas is intended to provide future specialist teachers with basic knowledge in the principal disciplines that comprise each subject as well as the necessary skills and abilities for applying this knowledge to the solution of problems. The major objective of training at this level is:

to make the students familiar with the interdependence of the individual disciplines involved, and with central terminology, procedures and methods as well as basic laws and relationships. The course provides the essential prerequisites for scientific classroom work..., training in methodology of the subject involved, and for further intense studies. Main emphasis is on ... disciplines that contribute to a deeper understanding of present and future subject matter to be taught at school.[18]

At the conclusion of the two-year period of fundamental education and training, the student is expected to have full mastery of the subject matter involved in all courses offered within the major and minor fields of specialty in the general and extended secondary schools.[19]

The final two-year period of specialist teacher training in the major and minor subject areas is characterized by intensive work in the major field of specialization and the methodology of teaching in the major and minor fields, an elective course, and extensive practice in the art of teaching. The elective course enables teacher aspirants to probe deeply into a specific area, or subdiscipline, of their major field and it provides "a survey of contents, methods, trends in research and development of that discipline."[20] Training in the methodology of teaching in the major and minor subject areas is based upon the knowledge, skills, and abilities acquired during the first stage of teacher training in pedagogy, psychology, and the major and minor fields of specialization and strives to consolidate, improve, and complete them.[21]

The mandatory programs according to which future specialist teachers of biology, chemistry, and physics are educated and trained have undergone extensive revision and updating in the past two years. These changes are reflected in current course requirements. The program of study for future teachers of biology is presented here for the purpose of illustrating the intensity of the training program required of specialist teachers in the GDR. Equally rigorous four-year study programs are required of future teachers specializing in other fields.

Students majoring in biology must successfully complete the following courses in partial fulfillment of the requirements for qualification as a specialist teacher in the field of biology: mathematical foundations for biology and chemistry instruction; introductory *Praktikum*, or laboratory, in physics; selected fundamental topics in chemistry; fundamental biology, special botany and zoology; plant physiology and biochemistry; the physiology of animals and human beings; ecology, socialist land development, and conservation; microbiology; genetics and the theory of evolution; and ideological-philosophical problems of natural science with an emphasis on biology.

TABLE 6-2[22]

Schedule of Courses Required for Future Teachers Whose Major Field of Specialization is Biology
(Cf. Table 6-1)

| | Semester[1] | | | | | | |
Course Title	1 L/S/P	2 L/S/P	3 L/S/P	4 L/S/P	5 L/S/P	6 L/S/P	7 L/S/P
2.1 Mathematical Foundations for Biology and Chemistry Instruction[2]	2/0/0						
2.2 Introductory *Praktikum* in Physics[2]		0/0/2					
2.3 Selected Fundamental Topics in Chemistry[3]	1/1/0						
2.4 Fundamental Biology[4]	4/2/3	0/0/3					
2.5 Special Botany and Zoology		3/0/2	2/1/0			1/1/1	
2.6 Plant Physiology and Biochemistry[5]			4/1/0	0/0/3	1/1/1		
2.7 The Physiology of Animals and Human Beings[5]				2/0/0	1/1/3		2/1/1
2.8 Ecology, Socialist Land Development, & Conservation			1/0/0	1/0/0		1/1/0	
2.9 Microbiology				1/0/0		1/0/2	
2.10 Genetics and the Theory of Evolution				1/1/0	1/0/0		1/0/1
2.11 Ideological-Philosophical Problems in Natural Science (Biology)							2/1/0

1) Notation: L = Lecture, S = Seminar, P = Laboratory *Praktikum*; numbers equal hours per week.

2) For students having major/minor combinations of biology/chemistry and chemistry/biology.

3) Only for students having major/minor combinations of biology/physical education and biology/friendship-Pioneer-leader training.

4) At the end of the first semester there is a one-week *Praktikum* for students with the major/minor combination of biology/chemistry and biology/physical education and a two-week *Praktikum* for students having the major/minor combination of friendship-Pioneer-leader training. For students having the major/minor combinations of biology/physical education and friendship-Pioneer-leader training/biology, the number of hours per week is the same as it is for students who have biology as a minor field of specialization (Cf. below, Table 6-3).

5) There is a one-week *Praktikum* at the end of the fifth semester for students majoring in biology.

TABLE 6-3[23]

Schedule of Courses for Future Teachers Whose Minor Field of Specialization is Biology
(Cf. Table 6-1)

Course Title	Semester[1]						
	1 L/S/P	2 L/S/P	3 L/S/P	4 L/S/P	5 L/S/P	6 L/S/P	7 L/S/P
2.1 Mathematical Foundations for Biology and Chemistry Instruction[2]	2/2/0						
2.2 Introductory *Praktikum* in Physics[2]		0/0/2					
2.3 Selected Fundamental Topics in Chemistry[3]	1/1/0						
2.4 Fundamental Biology[4]	3/2/3	1/0/3					
2.5 Special Botany and Zoology[5]		3/0/2	2/1/0				
2.6 Plant Physiology and Biochemistry			4/1/0	0/0/3			
2.7 The Physiology of Animals and Human Beings[6]				2/0/0	1/1/3		
2.8 Ecology, Socialist Land Development, & Conservation			1/0/0	1/0/0			
2.9 Microbiology[6]				1/0/0			
2.10 Genetics and the Theory of Evolution				1/1/0	1/0/0		

1) Notation: L = Lecture, S = Seminar, P = Laboratory-*Praktikum*; numbers equal hours per week.
2) For students having major/minor combinations of chemistry/biology and biology/chemistry.
3) Only for students having major/minor combinations of physical education/biology and geography/biology.
4) There is a one-week *Praktikum* at the end of the first semester for students with the major/minor combinations of chemistry/biology, physical education/biology, and geography/biology. The hours per week for students with the combination chemistry/biology is the same as for biology majors (Cf. Table 6-2).
5) A one-week *Praktikum* at the end of the third semester for the combination geography/biology.
6) A one-week *Praktikum* at the end of the fifth semester for the combinations physical education/biology, chemistry/biology, and geography/biology.

Teacher aspirants whose minor field of specialization is biology are required to complete the same courses as students whose major subject area is biology during the first two years of teacher-training; however, during the last two years of training, their courses in the field of biology are limited to the physiology of animals and human beings, and genetics and the theory of evolution.

Methods courses in biology are the same whether biology is the major or minor field of specialization. They are taken during the last five semesters of teacher training and include: theoretical foundations for formulating biology instruction; two courses entitled "School-practical exercises" in which teacher aspirants have the opportunity to study and practice the activities involved in teaching biology in the general and extended secondary schools; a (general) school biology *Praktikum* in which the theory and practical application of essential experimental techniques as well as the handling of instruments and preparation of instructional aids are treated; and thirteen weeks of practical biology teaching experience during the last semester of teacher training which also includes evaluation of the future biology teacher specialist.

Examinations in a specific subject are given at the end of a series of courses in that subject. A major examination is taken by all future specialist teachers at the end of the seventh semester and during the eighth semester of teacher training. Components of this examination are Marxist-Leninist theory, pedagogy and psychology, methodology of teaching the major and minor subject areas, and topics in the major field of specialization. The thesis required for qualification as a teacher for grades 5 through 12 must be completed during the eighth semester, and this "diploma paper" must be publicly defended at the conclusion of the eighth semester.[24]

Practice in working with children and young people is an aspect of specialist teacher preparation from the first semester of training. During the first two years of teacher training, the political-practical activity (*Cf. above, Table 6-1*) involves future specialist teachers in youth organizations and as leaders of amateur after-school groups. At the end of the first year of training, attendance at a practical course in summer holiday activities at a Pioneer camp (Pioneer camps are run under the auspices of the Young Pioneers, the Communist youth organization in the GDR) is required for the purpose of supplementing experiences with children gained during the year.

Observation of lessons taught by skilled and experienced teachers is a major component of a three-week practical course required during the third semester. The purpose of this course is to acquaint students

TABLE 6-4[25]

Schedule of Methodology Courses for Future Teachers Whose Major or Minor Field of Specialization is Biology

(Cf. Table 6-1)

Course Title	Semester[1]					Total Hours of Lecture	Seminar/ Exercises	Study Total
	4 L/S/P	5 L/S/P	6 L/S/P	7 L/S/P	8			
Theoretical Foundations for the Formulation of Biology Instruction	1/0/0[2]	1/1/0	1/1/0			47	32	79
Social-Practical Exercises		0/1/0		0/2/0		–	46	46
Large School-Praktikum including Evaluation					13 weeks			
School Biology Praktikum[3]			0/0/2			–	–	32

1) Notation: L = Lecture, S = Seminar or Exercises, P = Laboratory-Praktikum; numbers equal hours per week.
2) The distribution of hours is to be arranged with those of the other field in the major/minor combination so that lectures and seminars can be alternated.
3) These hours are placed at the disposal of the biology department.

with the work of specialist teachers in the general and extended secondary schools. The thirteen-week *Praktikum* is a major aspect of the eighth semester of training. Primary emphasis is on the future teacher's "largely independent handling of classroom work. The trainee teacher is now in complete charge of the lessons in the subject involved in one class, according to curriculum specifications."[26] An important aspect of this course is the evaluation that is made of the teacher trainee. Recent changes that have been made in the required curriculum for future teachers of the intermediary and secondary stages of compulsory education reflect an increase in the portion of time devoted to practicing the art of teaching under the supervision of trained specialist teachers.

It is apparent that the education and training of teachers in the GDR is purposeful and concise in that the course of study for future compulsory school specialist teachers is directly related to the teaching methodology and subject matter of the major and minor fields of concentration as they pertain to the ten-year general polytechnical secondary school. Additional courses in Marxist-Leninist philosophy and related areas of study serve to train future teachers to fulfill their obligation of contributing to the development of Communist conviction in GDR youth. In general, the close interrelation between the teacher-training programs and the curricula of the ten-year general polytechnical secondary schools promotes the effectiveness of the latter.

During the course of my residence in the GDR, I had the opportunity to meet with two teaching methodologists at the *Paedagogische Hochschule* "Karl Liebknecht" in the city of Potsdam. They were Professor Dr. Manfred Wuenschmann, a leading GDR methodologist in physics instruction and chairman of the department of Physics Teaching Methodology, and Dr. Helmut Barthel, deputy chairman of the department of Chemistry Teaching Methodology. Areas of discussion during our meeting of April 5, 1977, included current positions concerning the methodology of science instruction, mental development and science learning, variations in student ability, and recent changes that have been made in the basic program for training future specialist teachers.

The *Paedagogische Hochschule* "Karl Liebknecht," founded in 1948 and, in October, 1970, named after Karl Liebknecht, a German socialist and leader of the Spartacist uprising of 1919, is one of several universities in the GDR devoted to the education and training of specialist teachers for the ten-year general polytechnical secondary school. Potsdam, a picturesque city on the Havel River, is situated in a wooded area surrounded by lakes. It is historically famous as the permanent residence of the Hohenzollern dynasty between 1660 and 1918. In July, 1945, it was the site of the post-war Potsdam Conference. The palaces, which include the "Schloss Sans Souci," the "Stadtschloss," and the "Neues Palais" located on the grounds of the Park Sans Souci, were commissioned by Frederick the Great of Prussia in the mid-eighteenth century.[27] These grounds and buildings are now maintained by the GDR. The "Schloss Sans Souci" is a historical museum, and the smaller residences and other buildings on the grounds of Sans Souci serve various contemporary functions. The *Paedagogische Hochschule* "Karl Liebknecht" is located on the grounds of Sans Souci, and the university maintains several other buildings in the central area of Potsdam as well. My discussion with the science teaching methodologists took place in a relatively new building located just outside of the park grounds.

During the discussion, the following major points were made concerning recent developments in the methodology of science teaching:

1. An important thesis is that the intellectual activity of students is not directly related to specific teaching methods: each method can develop intellectual activity and no particular method is preferable. Teaching methodologists are, therefore, not presently concerned with the further systematization of teaching methods. However, great importance is currently being given to development of the application of all known methods to the instructional process for the purpose of increasing teaching effectiveness.

2. In Marxist-Leninist pedagogy, knowledge is divided into two areas: (1) *Sachwissen*, which includes knowledge of facts, laws, phenomena, et cetera; and, (2) *Methodenwissen*, or the knowledge of methods, i.e., models, relationships between models and reality. A basic position in the methodology of science teaching in the GDR is that the acquisition of factual knowledge requires a certain amount of memorization on the part of the students; thus, continual efforts are being made to combine the learning of facts with the process of cognition and to attain the optimum proportion between them. Science educators and methodologists in the GDR are of the opinion that overemphasis of the "process" or "inquiry" approach to learning science results in a lack of time for teaching the factual aspects of science knowledge. Learning by inquiry has a place in the total learning process, according to GDR science teaching methodologists, but it must be founded on the knowledge of facts, laws, and basic

research methods so that the inquiry has an organizational basis and is goal-oriented. In this way, discovery becomes a learning process.

3. Integration of experiments into the instructional period is a basic position of natural science instruction in GDR general schools. Experiments should be a part of the learning process and they should also contribute to arousing student curiosity and interest.

4. Recently developed science instruction methods books— *Methodik Biologieunterricht*, *Methodik Chemieunterricht*, and *Methodik Physikunterrricht* are viewed as signficant contributions to the development of the methodology of science teaching at the level of compulsory education in the GDR. A new book on the methodology of physics instruction has been written under the GDR leadership of Prof. Dr. Wuenschmann in cooperation with physics instruction methodologists in the Soviet Union.

New developments in the methodology of physics instruction appearing in the book by Wuenschmann *et al.* include: (1) greater organization of the learning process during instructional periods; (2) increased emphasis on the philosophical foundations of the learning process and a de-emphasis of the psychological foundations of learning (in the view of pedagogical scientists in the GDR, the psychological approach to learning theory is too narrow); (3) a change in educational elements to increase subject matter relevance; and (4) an effort has been made to increase the "inner compactness" and logical structure of individual topic areas. These new developments, which are the bases of the science teaching methodology books, have been integrated into the courses in biology, chemistry, and physics teaching methodology offered by the universities. They will become operative at the level of the general schools when the current specialist teacher aspirants complete their training and begin working as specialist teachers in biology, chemistry, and physics.

5. In response to my observation concerning the absence of student-originated questions during the instructional periods observed at the Sixth *Polytechnische Oberschule* in the Berlin district of Weissensee, the methodologists acknowledged the existence of shortcomings in student abilities to join discussions and ask questions. Since the quantity and quality of student questions is a criterion for evaluating teaching effectiveness, considerable work is needed, according to them, in finding ways of stimulating the student question process.

6. The use of television broadcasts during instructional periods is being introduced in science courses in the general schools. Advantages of occasionally using television as an instructional aid are (1) experiments can be shown which individual schools are not equipped to

undertake and (2) subject areas can be enriched through different approaches to teaching as well as through cartooned presentations and other techniques that foster the development of student interest. In addition to this use of instructional television, public television in the GDR broadcasts programs specifically designed to supplement science instruction in the general schools as well as programs to aid science teachers in the development of their teaching methodology.

The best works in the field of contemporary educational psychology, according to the methodologists, are those of Galperin, Leontiew *et al.*, of the Soviet Union. The basic theory of their work is that the ability to perform intellectual activities develops in stages. It is this approach to the development of the human intellect that is included in the psychology courses required during specialist teacher training.

Critical studies of the developmental theories of Jean Piaget have been undertaken in the GDR, particularly by Krueger, Lomscher *et al.*, who have studied children in kindergarten and first grade. In general, however, Piaget's theories are not much esteemed by GDR pedagogical scientists, since they have determined that children have greater intellectual capabilities at an earlier age than suggested by Piaget. The prevalent view among GDR educators is that psychology is not ready to set a basis, or schedule, for curriculum development. In the GDR, curriculum development and its relation to the level of intellectual development of the students is based upon experimental results and experiences.

The grade level at which specific courses are introduced depends on the intellectual development of the students, Thus, for example, the natural sciences are taught propaedeutically during the first four grades. According to pedagogical scientists in the GDR, student abilities for abstract thinking and systematization are not sufficiently developed prior to the fifth or sixth grades to warrant studying sciences as separate course-developed subjects. No present efforts are, therefore, being made in the GDR to introduce science courses into the lower grades (one through four) of compulsory education. It was noted, however, that in Hungary experiments and investigations are being made regarding the introduction of a general science course during the first four grades of the Hungarian equivalent of the GDR general schools.

In this connection, it was stated that at present there is no thought of changing the structure of contemporary curricula in the natural sciences. Efforts are being made, however, to gain the greatest learning effectiveness within the context of the present curriculum structure.

A current topic being considered by GDR educators concerns the possibility of making the selection of a *Rahmenprogramm fuer Arbeitsgemeinschaften* (Cf. below, page 120) mandatory for all ninth and tenth grade students in the ten-year general polytechnical secondary school.

Pedagogical scientists in the GDR recognize that different abilities and skills exist among students in the general schools. They also consider, however, that there is no limit to the development of the individual. In general, every person is conceived as being capable of increasing his or her level of knowledge.

According to GDR educators, it is a false notion that a particular student can learn history and be unable to understand the natural sciences: all students are capable of understanding science. In this connection it was pointed out that, commensurate with efforts to aid physically and psychologically handicapped children in fulfilling compulsory education requirements, science courses are being taught in the special schools with considerable success. If science can be taught to psychologically handicapped children, the obvious conclusion is that children who are sufficiently healthy to attend the general schools are capable of understanding it.

Important considerations for teaching any subject in the general schools are the selection of relevant topics, the achievement of proper levels of simplification of subject matter, correct training of teachers, and effective application of teaching methodology. These efforts are being significantly promoted by attempts to equalize instruction through use of compulsory curricula in all subjects, textbooks that correspond exactly to the compulsory curricula, and *Unterrichtshilfen*, or guide books for teachers.

In the coming years, efforts will be made to expand and increase the effectiveness of *Unterrichtshilfen* in current use so that science teachers will have complete plans from which to teach for each instructional period. An advantage of this approach towards the equalization of teacher effectiveness is that science teachers will be provided with the best possible material and techniques for teaching the required subject matter. The disadvantage, however, is that *Unterrichtshilfen* tend to inhibit development of the art of teaching by constricting teachers to one manner of approach. Thus, an essential consideration in the development of the new *Unterrichtshilfen* will be to find more ways of motivating teacher creativity.

New study schedules for the training of specialist teachers in biology, chemistry, and physics for the general schools will be instituted this year in all GDR universities responsible for this aspect of higher education. Changes that have been made in the basic program for *all* specialist teacher aspirants include the following:[28]

1. The number of hours per week of instruction in Marxism-Leninism have been changed to give the subject greater emphasis in the third and fourth years than in the first two years. The total formal instruction time has been increased by approximately fourteen hours.

2. The total number of hours of formal instruction in pedagogy and psychology have been increased by sixty-two; an increase that is reflected mainly in the second stage of specialist teacher training.

3. Methodology courses in the major and minor fields of specialization will begin in the fourth rather than in the fifth semester. The total number of hours of formal instruction in teaching methodology have been increased by thirty.

4. Russian language instruction has been extended to the third semester and the total number of hours of formal instruction has been increased by fifteen.

5. Three courses have been added to the first stage of teacher training: Speech Training (twelve hours of total instruction time); Techniques of Working with Audio-Visual Instructional Aids (sixteen hours); and Cultural-Aesthetic Education and Training (thirty-two hours).

A new course has been added to the study program in the seventh semester for students majoring in biology, chemistry, or physics. The course, comprised of thirty instructional periods, is entitled "Ideological-Philosophical Problems of Natural Science" with an emphasis on biology, chemistry, or physics depending on the specialist teacher aspirant's major field of specialization. The structure of this course in chemistry and physics is similar and includes the following major topic areas: the relationship between Marxist-Leninist philosophy and natural science; the Marxist-Leninist concept of matter and its significance for the specific science, e.g., chemistry or physics; the materialist dialectic and chemistry, or physics; and, philosophical problems of the knowledge acquisition processes in chemistry and physics. An additional topic area in the chemistry oriented course is entitled "The Science of Chemistry and its Social Character." Topic areas included in the biology variant of this course are: the social determinism of science; the relationship between philosophy and natural science; materialism and objective dialectics of life; theory of knowledge foundations for biology; the human individual as a biological and social being; and, the relationship between society and biology in the epoch of transition from capitalism to socialism.[29]

As a final comment, the methodologists noted that it has become necessary for the GDR to increase its total number of teachers. These new requirements are the result of recently initiated social-political measures such as a reduction in the total number of instructional periods that a teacher is required to teach, giving single teachers over forty years of age one day off per month for housekeeping purposes, et cetera. In the district of Potsdam alone, for example, an increase of 4,000 teachers will be necessary in the near future.

CHAPTER VII

INSIDE AN EAST GERMAN SCHOOL

The following is a report of my visit to the Sixth Ten-Year General Polytechnical Secodary School of the city district, Weissensee, in East Berlin on March 29, 1977. In evaluating the perceptions gained, due consideration must be given to the pitfalls inherent in generalizing from the specific to the universal, that is, in applying impressions gained from a day-long visit to one general school to all general schools. These pitfalls are diminished to relatively "safe" proportions, however, as a consequence of the uniformity prevalent in GDR compulsory education. The extent of this uniformity was recently summed up by an official of the GDR Ministry of Education as follows: with due regard for the factors of variation in teacher personality and the differing ages of school buildings, one can safely say that observing classes being taught in one general school is tantamount to observing these same classes in any other general school, since the teachers must follow the prescribed curricula and textbooks and as a result of the uniform approach to training teachers.[1]

The assumption can be made that the school chosen by GDR officials for this visit is above average. It must be understood, however, that in GDR socialist society, the range of difference between the best and the most disadvantaged general schools is relatively small. Many general school buildings are more modern than the Sixth Ten-Year General Polytechnical Secondary School in Weissensee. I was told that all general schools have equally well-equipped facilities for science teaching, although other schools are not as well equipped for teaching other subject areas. Another consideration to be taken into account is that the Sixth Polytechnical Secondary School is located in a major city which is considered to be the capitol of the GDR. Thus, one would expect to find a more cosmopolitan atmosphere in this school than in a general school located in a small rural village. This consideration must be balanced, however, by recognition of the fact that the GDR is very proud that it has achieved virtual equality of educational opportunity in all general schools regardless of their location in rural or urban environments. As a final comment, at the close of my visit a science teacher in our discussion group spontaneously remarked that the lessons that had been observed were "absolutely typical" of the manner in which science is taught in general schools throughout the GDR—a remark with with the other teachers present were in total agreement.

In the GDR, science education is an integral aspect of the total scope of compulsory education and training. The development and training of socialist personality characteristics anchored on the foundation of socialist morality in GDR youth is a vital aspect of this compulsory education. It is essential, therefore, to describe the science instruction observed within the framework of a description of the total educational environment as I perceived it.

The school is the Sixth Ten-Year General Polytechnical Secondary School at Langhansstrasse 120 in the Berlin district of Weissensee: an urban area of small shops, light industry, warehouses, and large apartment buildings located three or four miles northeast of the city's commercial center known as Alexanderplatz. The school building is an old, large-windowed, three-storied structure that predates World War One. The age of the building enhances the sense of interest because of its architectural individuality in comparison to the uniform construction of the newer general school buildings, and from a moment's pause for reflection on the educational systems that have been contained within its walls, each in the service of the then-extant political system: the social-democratic Weimar Republic, the era of Nazi fascism, and the contemporary period of Marxist-Leninist socialism. The current system of education represents a radical step in the evolution of German education. The traditional elitist approach, whereby academic education was reserved largely for the privileged minority and vocational education was the lot of the masses, has been replaced by the egalitarian approach embodied in a uniform, ten-year compulsory general education for all children. This system of education strives to instill a love for physical labor in young people, and views the still-apparent preference for intellectually oriented work as a vestige from capitalism that must be eliminated in socialist society.

It is 7:45 a.m. and I am met at the school's front entrance by the director, a hospitable, middle-aged woman, who welcomes me to Weissensee's Sixth Ten-Year General Polytechnical Secondary School with a bouquet of red and white carnations. The visit itself, as has already been noted, is not a mundane event. Although many visitors and observers from the socialist and developing countries pass through the GDR general schools, this is the first official visit to this school by an American. In the course of a brief conversation in the director's office, I am informed that two physics courses and two chemistry classes have been selected for observation to be followed by a discussion session with the science teachers in the director's office.

Nearly six hundred students attend the Sixth Polytechnical Secondary School which has been named the Grete Walter *Polytechnische Oberschule*. The director is eager to inform me about Grete Walter and the role that her memory plays in the life of the school; this information is readily available on the posters displayed in the school's front entrance hall. Grete Walter was a young Communist who was arrested and tortured by the Nazis for her anti-fascist activities and who, in 1935 at the age of twenty-two, committed suicide in prison. Her revolutionary zeal and devotion to the cause of communism are among the reasons that her memory is thus honored.

The purpose of memorializing Grete Walter is the vital and inspirational one of presenting the school's student body with a heroic Communist figure with whom to identify and, thus, to assist in the development of productive socialist student personalities. Identification is sought through interaction with her living relatives. Student identification with Grete Walter is also sought by integrating her memory into the activities of the school; thus, for example, the students are urged to honor her by striving for scholastic excellence, by assisting in the maintenance and development of school property, by striving to emulate her socialist personality traits, and so on. It should be noted that this specific case can be generalized to the majority of general schools in the GDR: it is a general policy that all schools strive to fulfill the requirements necessary for being granted the name of a prominent Communist or non-Communist personality. Naming a school is not an act *pro forma*, but, rather, the name that a school carries plays an active role in pedagogical efforts towards the development of socialist consciousness in the student body as a whole.

The large schoolyard of the Grete Walter *Polytechnische Oberschule* is not visible from the street and is surrounded on three sides by the U-shaped school. Inside, the halls and classrooms are light and airy. There is a sense of disciplined informality; between classes, the hallways are crowded with students ranging in age from six to seventeen years. As the director moves through the halls, occasional students turn to greet her and, if she perceives behavior unfitting to the school environment, she moves in unhesitatingly to correct it.

The physical surroundings are old and neat. Occasional student-painted murals in various stages of completion adorn the walls in the halls and stairwells. One very colorful mural depicts Soviet astronauts maneuvering outside their space ship far above the surface of the earth.

Students carry their jackets or coats and *Schulmappen* (rucksack-style briefcases) with them between class periods. The director explains that financial resources are not presently available for constructing student coat cabinets, however, the possibility exists that the school's basement may be developed for that purpose according to the model of many schools in the Soviet Union. For the present, the students seem to manage easily; during the recess breaks, their *Schulmappen* are stacked in piles at *FDJ-Kontrollposten* (areas in school hallways monitored by members of the *Freie Deutsche Jugend*, the Communist youth organization in the GDR).

The director informs me that in this school all subjects studied by students in the fifth through the tenth grades are taught in *Fachuntrrichtsraueme*. Chemistry, physics, and biology are taught in specially equipped classroom laboratories in all ten-year general polytechnical secondary schools.

The current educational goal is to equip every GDR general school with specialized classrooms for all subjects taught between the fifth and tenth grades. Classes comprising the first four grades are taught by teachers who are responsible for teaching all subjects to the class with the frequent exception of sports, music, and art, when specialist teachers in these areas are available. Thus, for the most part, pupils in the first four grades remain in one classroom during the course of a school day. For students in the fifth grade and above, however, the concept of learning in *Fachunterrichtsraueme* requires that they move from room to room during the course of a school day, while the specialist teacher tends to teach all classes in the same classroom laboratory.

Each grade is divided into individual classes of approximately twenty-six students. (According to GDR laws and regulations, the maximum number of pupils allowable in a class is thirty and the eventual goal is to reduce the number of students per class to twenty.) In response to a question concerning the manner in which a typical class is formed, the director stated that when a new group of students enters the first grade, individual classes are constructed on the basis of reports accompanying the children from kindergartens and the occupations of their parents. The goal is to equally distribute the children of workers and intellectuals as well as children with desirable and undesirable personality characteristics among the classes. In general, a class that is established in the first grade progresses through the ten-year period of compulsory education as a unit. Occasional students are gained and lost as a result of family moves. Usually from one to three students are selected to attend the extended secondary school at the end of the eighth grade and an additional student leaves school after the eighth grade to begin a three-year period of vocational training—including general education—because of an inability to successfully fulfill academic requirements in the general school.

A class remains a basically cohesive learning unit throughout the ten-year period of mandatory education in the GDR and is called a learning collective. A learning collective is viewed as contributing importantly to the healthy development of the socialist student personality since developing personalities are able to interact and grow over a relatively long period of time in a known and, therefore, stable social environment. Such an environment is conducive to the amelioration of excessive individualism as well as to the integration of student thinking towards a more collective orientation.

The school day in the ten-year general polytechnical secondary school begins at 8 a.m. For fifth through tenth graders, the school day extends until 2 p.m. six days per week, Mondays through Saturdays. Class periods are forty-five minutes long and the class periods are separated by ten-minute intervals except for a twenty-minute recess in the school yard for eating snacks brought from home between the second and third periods and a half-hour lunch break between the fourth and fifth periods. Pupils in the seventh through tenth grades spend one day each week in a school-associated industry during which time they receive polytechnical instruction and training. After school there are extracurricular activities in which students can elect to participate and, in addition, considerable homework is normally assigned.

Science classes are taught in rooms that serve the combined function of classroom and laboratory. These classroom laboratories are specially equipped for teaching the specific subjects of biology, chemistry, and physics; in the Sixth *Polytechnische Oberschule*, astronomy is taught in a mathematics *Fachunterrichtsraum*.

The classroom laboratories are adequate in size and accommodate approximately twenty-one laboratory tables, each suitable for two students; a teacher's demonstration table; and cabinets for storing laboratory equipment, various teaching aids adapted to the subject matter, and an overhead projector and screen (*Figure 7-1*). Each *Fachunterrichtsraum* is adjoined by a teacher workroom, although occasionally one workroom is shared by teachers from two classroom laboratories devoted to the same subject. A typical science teacher's workroom contains a desk and cabinets for storing laboratory equipment and supplies as well as various instructional aids and reference books.

The classes selected by the director for observation were a ninth grade chemistry class, a tenth grade physics laboratory, a sixth grade physics class, and an eighth grade chemistry class. My impression was positive, and resulted from the realization that the study of these science subjects is an experience required of all general school students who appeared earnest during the instructional period. Another major positive impression concerned the extent to which teacher instruction and student activity in the form of teacher-directed, question-and-answer repartee and student experiments were integrated into the teaching-learning process during a class period.

Each of the three instructional periods observed began with the introduction of new subject matter by means of the teacher's brief reference to the topic followed by a lively session of teacher-posed questions. The questions had the dual purpose of consolidating previously acquired knowledge and arousing interest in the new topic: the teacher's questions required the students to apply their knowledge to the formulation of answers concerning the new subject. This introductory process consumed approximately five minutes of class time and concluded when the teacher had ascertained that some of the pupils were successful in making valid general deductions on the basis of previously acquired information for the purpose of explaining the new phenomenon.

The teacher next sought to reinforce these deductions by means of a demonstration experiment. This procedure initiated the treatment or processing of new subject matter. Observations resulting from the demonstration led to further teacher-posed questions for the purpose of refining previous generalizations made by the students. The teacher's questions were followed by an explanation of the new phenomenon accomplished by means of the creative integration of the following didactic forms: (1) an informal teacher-lecture which included writing relevant information on a green colored chalk board and on a transparency for overhead projection, (2) the question-and-answer form during which time the teacher formulated questions designed to guide student concept formation as well as to determine

FIGURE 7-1

Schematic Diagram of a *Fachunterrichtsraum*, or *Kabinett*,
and the Adjoining Teacher's Workroom

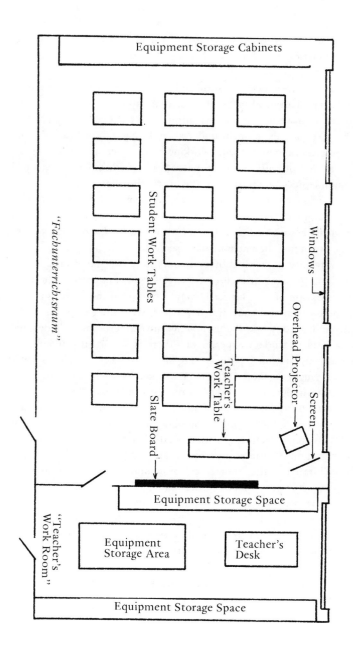

teaching effectiveness on the basis of student comprehension, and (3) independent student activity in the form of experimentation.

The final portion of each of the observed instructional periods was devoted to the consolidation of knowledge of the new subject matter acquired during the course of the class period. This instructional function was accomplished by different methods in each of the classes observed as follows:

1. a teacher-guided, question-and-answer session for the purpose of relating theoretical material presented earlier in the period to the practical utilization of this information in the GDR national economy;

2. a student experiment undertaken during the final twenty minutes of class time by students working either alone or in pairs for the purpose of reproducing results theoretically predicted and developed during the preceding portion of the instructional period; and

3. a relatively more complex teacher demonstration experiment which required the students to consolidate information acquired during the course of the instructional period for the purpose of correctly explaining the phenomena observed.

The facility with which experiments were integrated into the instructional process in each of these classes was impressive. It was a demonstration of the Marxist-Leninist concept of the unity of theory and practice in the educational process. With the exception of the ninth and tenth grade *Praktika* which involve class periods devoted completely to student experiments, there is no formal scheduling of separate instructional periods and laboratory sessions for science courses taught in the GDR general schools. Rather, student experiments are integrated into the instructional process. The concept of the *Fachunterrichtsraum* is conducive to this approach to science education, since such rooms are designed for the combined functions of classroom instruction and student laboratory work.

Integration of teacher instruction and student experimentation is also facilitated by the arrangement of laboratory equipment in easily accessible storage cabinets in the rear of the *Fachunterrichtsraum* and by the level of student discipline observed. Each pair of students has a box of standard equipment related to the subject area under current discussion which is stored in the cabinets and which they are responsible for taking out prior to the beginning of class and putting away at the end of the period. This process was accomplished quickly and quietly by the students, and without explicit instructions from the teacher. Special laboratory equipment and supplies are set out on the student work tables by the teacher prior to the start of class and are collected by the teacher at the conclusion of the period. The teacher is responsible for the safe functioning of laboratory and demonstration equipment and for safe student use of electrical equipment and chemicals.

The reason stated by the director for selecting the sixth grade physics class for observation was to show how children are introduced to the process of experimentation. The purpose of the physics lesson observed was to teach the concept of electrical charge on the basis of an elementary concept of atomic structure.

When the students arrived in the *Fachunterrichtsraum*, each student's work space was supplied with a plastic rod and a simple electroscope. The subject matter was introduced by the teacher-directed method of question-and-answer and teacher-demonstration experiment to ascertain the transformation of electrical energy. The teacher then suggested that the students rub the plastic rod on their clothes after which the rod was to be brought to the measuring instrument (the teacher did not refer to the electroscope by name). A theoretical explanation of the resulting observations, excellently directed to the developmental level of sixth grade pupils, was given by the teacher in combination with the method of question-and-answer to aid the students in the processing of knowledge and to reinforce his theoretical explanation.

Next, the teacher suggested that the students attempt to pick up a tiny bit of paper with the plastic rod after rubbing it on their sleeves. The students observed that the paper stuck to the rod. The teacher asked why this happened. Some students said that it was an effect of magnetism. The teacher rejected this reply and asked if it could possibly be magic. "No," replied the students. "Well, what is it," asked the teacher, "heat?" The students rejected this explanation and some responded that it was a phenomenon of electrical charge. The teacher next charged a pair of metal spheres to show the effects of electrical charge, attraction and repulsion. Observations and questions posed by the teacher led the students to deduce that like charges repel and unlike charges attract. Student interest had now been aroused to a higher level than was apparent at the start of class and the students became very interested in explaining the observed phenomenon and appeared anxious to answer questions.

After an intensive period of question-and-answer and teacher demonstration, the teacher offered a more detailed explanation of what had occurred with the aid of a schematic diagram of an atom and a listing of important points projected on the overhead viewer.

The teacher's explanation was followed by a more complex experiment in which a free-swinging charged metal sphere was placed between two non-parallel plates of opposite charge. In order to explain the phenomenon which caused the metal sphere to swing back and forth between the plates, the students were required to consolidate information acquired earlier in the period. Explanations were offered, but the teacher did not find them to be explicit enough. Within a short time, however, one student succeeded in explaining exactly what had occurred in the demonstration; the teacher's pleasure was obvious and the student was well commended for his success.

As a conclusion to the instructional work undertaken during the class period, the teacher placed a smoke-producing candle underneath a hollow tube, held vertically, through which a wire was passed. When the wire was charged, no smoke came out of the top of the tube. The teacher explained the phenomenon with reference to the previous demonstration and stated that it was the principle of the electric gas cleaner which was important for environmental protection, particularly in large cities and industrial complexes. In this manner, the entire preceding discussion was made relevant.

Another physics class that I observed was the second period of the tenth grade physics *Praktikum*. It was explained that in the tenth grade physics course, students are responsible for carrying out ten laboratory experiments in addition to the regular student experiments that are integrated into the instructional period. Fifteen experiments which are representative of the major areas of physics that have been studied from the sixth grade through the first half of the tenth grade have been designed and published under the title *Physik 10 Praktikum*.[2] In the second half of the tenth grade physics course, the teacher selects ten of these experiments which all students are required to complete. Each experiment must be finished during the course of a forty-five minute class period. During each period, ten different experiments are set up at separate work tables and a schedule is composed by the teacher so that each group of three students will have worked through each experiment at the end of ten instructional periods. Student work groups are established by the students before the start of the ten-hour *Praktikum*.

Laboratory work proceeds independently of the teacher who is present as a cooperative guide in the event of special problems that the students might encounter, but, otherwise, keeps communication to a minimum. Laboratory worksheets are prepared by the students prior to arrival in class. The work must be completed and written up in forty-five minutes and submitted to the teacher at the conclusion of the period. The individual groups of students are graded on their work as a unit, and each student in the group receives the same grade on an experiment.

The atmosphere in the *Fachunterrichtsraum* throughout the period was one of diligent earnestness directed towards the laboratory work. Low voice levels and purposeful manual movements were noted. Each student was aided in his or her work by a book of mathematical tables and a slide rule. The students exhibited facility in the use of both, and both were in continued use. I was informed that use of the slide rule is initiated in seventh grade mathematics; thereafter, its utilization is integrated into the educational program of the general schools. The testing of student physics laboratory skills and knowledge of physics experiments is an aspect of the final examination in tenth grade physics. In one section of the final examination, each student is required to independently set up the equipment for and carry out an experiment selected by the teacher.

As the students worked, the director informed me of a basic purpose of the physics *Praktika* (in addition to the tenth grade *Praktikum*, there is a six-hour *Praktikum* in the ninth grade) and *Praktika* in other science subjects: through the aegis of collective fulfillment of prescribed tasks, they contribute importantly to the development of desirable, socialist personality characteristics. At the conclusion of the tenth grade, all students in the ten-year polytechnical secondary school begin a two-year period of vocational education and training, except for the less than ten percent of the students who enter three-year vocational schools in which vocational training is combined with academic work and culminates in vocational qualification and the *Abitur*. The *Praktika* in physics and the other natural sciences are, therefore, viewed as an important bridge connecting school with the reality of industrial and agricultural work in socialist society where collectives of varying size are responsible for the effective accomplishment of work goals. The interaction of the individual with the collective in the ninth and tenth grade physics *Praktika* promotes the development of desirable socialist personality characteristics such as conscientiousness, mutual respect, and assistance in the cooperative fulfillment of common tasks. These traits are deemed essential to the effective functioning of socialist agriculture and industry.

During observation of student experiments in each class, it was noted that the students approached their work in a quiet and intent manner; that equipment was handled with smooth, purposeful motions, and that each piece of equipment was carefully put aside when not in use. The director commented that the development of this approach is begun in the first grade. The extent to which this training has been successful is indicated by the fact that even during the laboratory portions of final examinations in the upper grades, when the students work without apparent supervision in the laboratory, it has been observed that the students approach their experimental work in exactly the same manner. The implication intended by this comment was that by the end of the period of compulsory education in the GDR, the careful approach to manual work in which the students had been training—exemplified in the student approach to natural science experiments observed—had been developed in the students to the level of a conditioned response which would probably remain characteristic of their approach to manual work in the future.

At the conclusion of a four-hour period of observation, the science teachers and I were invited to the director's office where a lively discussion followed around a table invitingly set with coffee and snacks. Major topics of discussion included: (1) the capability of all students to fulfill science requirements in the ten-year general polytechnical secondary school; (2) the extracurricular science activities that are available to general school students; (3) the method by which students who are highly talented in the area of the natural sciences are identified; and (4) the role of science education in the ten-year general polytechnical secondary school of the GDR.

The question was asked whether all students who are involved in compulsory education in the general schools are capable of fulfilling the requirements imposed by six years of mandatory study of biology, five years of physics, four years of chemistry, and one year of astronomy. The reply was as follows: It is not a question of whether this or that student is capable of the work prescribed; of course all physically and psychologically healthy children are capable of studying and learning the natural sciences. The point is that the work is necessary and, therefore, required. Thus, the question is one of finding the most effective way of fulfilling the task of educating the nation's youth in natural science.

A prime motivation for science education is the fact that science is the force by which the national economy of the GDR is guided and developed; in the GDR, the trend is towards the development of so-called "skilled-work-intensive" and "science-intensive" industries in contrast to industries that are dependent on the consumption of great quantities of materials. The GDR is a small country: its total land area is 108,178 square kilometers and, in 1975, its population was 16,820,000.[3] Given its small size, its state of economic devastation at the end of World War II, and the fact that it inherited the least economically viable portion of pre-war Germany, the GDR has accomplished a major feat by developing its economic status to that of the tenth leading industrial nation of the world. This feat of economic development is in large part attributed to the socialist system of general education that has been developed in the GDR since 1945.

As a result of the GDR's relatively poor endowment of natural resources, the present rate of economic development can continue only if concomitant efforts are made to intensify science education at the level of the general schools as the basis for productive activity in all spheres of technology and to serve as the foundation on which to build a Marxist-Leninist world view and Communist conviction. Therefore, all youth in the GDR are required to study the natural sciences. The polytechnical approach to this task is considered by Communist educators to be the most effective method of teaching science that has been developed to date. Within the framework of this approach, however, continual efforts are being made to elevate the level of science education in the GDR.

The prevalent theory underlying science learning is that "interest in science comes from learning science" and interest motivates learning. In Communist pedagogy, motivation is a corollary of academic achievement. Levels of learning achievement are recognized within the classroom learning collective by a grading system in which the highest learning achievement is rewarded with a grade of "1" and the lowest passing level with a grade of "4." Failure to fulfill course requirements is graded with a "5," although, according to the spirit of the collective, the necessity of awarding any student a failing grade must be viewed as a failure of the collective effort.

Final grades in science courses are based on grades given by the teacher during the course of the school year for work done on exercises, experiments, written lessons and assignments, and classroom participation, as well as a written examination given in May and an oral examination given in June. The purpose of both final examinations is to evaluate the student's level of comprehension of subject matter taught during the course of the year. The examinations are designed and approved at the state level and arrive in the teacher's hands in sealed envelopes on examination day. The science grades that a student accumulates over a period of time are indicative of the student's level of scientific achievement, which is construed to be a register of scientific interest and motivation. It was generally agreed, by the science teachers and the director, that the most common cause of low motivation and, hence, of low grades, is a deficient home environment, i.e., one that is not conducive to the development of an interest in learning.

Just as in extracurricular activities in general, extracurricular science activities are intended for student participation at the conclusion of formal classes at 2 p.m. on weekday afternoons. These activities are organized by the local director of extracurricular activities for the purpose of serving student interests. In comparison to instructional period activities which are teacher-directed, students are the source and center of extracurricular activities.

In grades 1 through 10, informal interest groups called *Arbeitsgemeinschaften* are formed on the basis of diverse and approved student interests, which frequently include science oriented interests. In the ninth and tenth grades, a more formal and serious form of extracurricular activity, called *Rahmenprogramme fuer Arbeitsgemeinschaften*, are offered for interested students in areas of the natural and social sciences. (These programs were initiated in 1970 and it is to be noted that since the introduction of the *Rahmenprogramme*, 60 percent of all ninth and tenth grade students in the general schools have chosen to participate in this form of extracurricular activity.) Among the *Rahmenprogramme* in which the ninth and tenth grade students can participate are extracurricular learning activities in microbiology, metallurgy, the atomic structure of matter, chemical technology, applied chemistry, electronics, and selected problems in environmental construction.[4] Science teachers are pleased with the spontaneous student response and interest in science oriented *Arbeitsgemeinschaften*, in general. An educational goal in the GDR is to make the selection of a *Rahmenprogramm* in the ninth and tenth grades obligatory for all general school students.

The factors of the GDR's limited size and population and its general deficiency of natural resources, combined with its ambitious economic objectives, makes the early discovery of youthful talent, particularly in the natural sciences and science-related areas, mandatory. The point is to discover it and then to encourage its development, according to the science teachers.

A method that has been effectively utilized for the discovery of science-talented youth is that of annual national competitions in the natural sciences and mathematics, called *Olympiaden*. The goals and range of the science competitions vary. On the district level, for example, they can be directed by the district's adviser for a specific natural science for the purpose of evaluating the necessity of improving the instructional level of that science in the district. The annual science *Olypiaden* in physics, chemistry, and mathematics, presently promoted by the universities and pedagogical institutes in the GDR, are organized for the purpose of discovering scientific talent. These competitions occur in successive rounds in which local finalists are encouraged to compete at the district level, district finalists at the next highest level, and so on, to the level of national competition. Winners of the national science competitions have the possibility of competing internationally with finalists from other—generally socialist—nations.

A point system for the annual science competitions has been developed and is used in all *Olympiaden* for the purpose of making comparisons and diagnostic statements regarding scientific talent.[5] Youth who have been discovered to be highly talented in the natural sciences are offered the possibility of continuing their compulsory education in specialized schools where, in addition to the mandatory curriculum of the ten-year general polytechnical secondary school, the study of specific natural sciences is accelerated and intensified for the purpose of presenting gifted youth with continual challenges aimed at developing their talent. Attendance at specialized natural science schools, however, is not required of *Olympiaden* finalists; they may elect to return to their neighborhood general school.

Science education in the general schools is based on the conviction that there is a narrow connection between science and life: natural science is the force that moves society forward. A major objective of the ten-year general polytechnical secondary school is to educate and train students so that upon completion of the requirements of compulsory education they are conversant with the laws of natural science and the Marxist-Leninist "laws" of social science to the extent that they can integrate the use of these laws into everyday life and, thereby, render their adult lives more effective and meaningful. The purpose of the natural science teacher is (1) to develop various scientific and technological abilities in students; (2) to awaken scientific and technological interests and talents in students and develop them sufficiently so that they will remain an active and motivating force throughout life; and, (3) to overcome residual fear, as it were, of technology so that the students, as adult men and women, will be able to make simple household repairs of a technological nature independently.

The science teachers remarked that the scientific interests of girls and boys are encouraged with equal vigor and that, on the basis of experience, it is observed that the scientific performance of girls is equal to and often better than that of boys at the level of the general schools. It was stressed, furthermore, that in contemporary GDR society, jobs in science and technology and related areas are open with equal opportunity to men and women alike.

On the basis of my observations and discussions, a general conclusion is that the total school environment in the Grete Walter *Polytechnische Oberschule* is conducive to learning the natural sciences. It is to be emphasized, however, that this is an assessment of the extant learning atmosphere and is not to be construed as a comment on the competence of this learning environment to foster future scientific creativity. In this regard, GDR educators are of the conviction that the purpose of education in the ten-year general polytechnical secondary school is to give a basic general education on which to build future interest, activity, and creativity for all children.

My impressions concerning the ability of this general school to provide its students with a basic scientific education are positive. The *Fachunterrichtsraueme*, or *Kabinette*, are well equipped and conducive to student experimentation and the general atmosphere pervading the school is one supportive of learning. On the basis of student behavior, it is apparent that the teachers are respected by the students and that, at least in the cases observed, the students have a warm and friendly relationship with the teacher. This student-teacher atmosphere was manifested in the observation of groups of students having conversations with the teachers prior to the start of the class period, in the interaction of the teacher with the students during the instructional period, and in the warm and sensitive manner in which the science teachers spoke about their students in later conversations with the investigator.

The science lessons that I observed were excellent illustrations of the concept of teaching as an art. The teaching methods used—creatively combined and approached with the proper degree of sensitivity for the ages of the students—aroused student curiosity and interest and evolved into a concentrated learning experience for the group, culminating in moments of insight by occasional students that were shared with the collective through the auspices of the teacher. My positive impressions of these science lessons were enhanced by the realization that the pupils addressed represented a spectrum of intellectual abilities and interests and that these learning experiences in natural science were mandatory for all children. A single negative impression resulted from the absence of questions posed by the students during the instructional periods observed.

The activities I observed in the *Fachunterrichtsraueme* of the Grete Walter *Polytechnische Oberschule* are products of teacher skill and interest. They are, however, also products of the discreet application of results of pedagogical research and the careful, goal-oriented planning that goes into all aspects of the system of general education in the GDR to make it an integrated whole and purposefully related to life in socialist society. Successful discharge of the tasks of compulsory education is, in the final analysis, a consequence of the training provided for teacher aspirants. In the area of the natural sciences, the successful attainment of educational objectives is dependent upon the education and training of science teachers. Teacher training in the GDR is based upon a basic knowledge of subject matter in the areas of specialization and upon a pedagogy that is contemporarily appraised as optimal within the given social context.

The obvious advantage of the degree of educational planning practiced in the GDR for teachers in general is that it provides them with a definitive knowledge concerning what they are expected to teach and how they are expected to approach the subject matter, thus, yielding time for developing the art of teaching. On the basis of my observations, it is apparent that the science teachers adhered strictly to the prescribed curricula and recommended teaching methodologies. It is also apparent, however, that rigid adherence to the rules surrounding teaching in the GDR can be most easily achieved by teachers who have strong Marxist-Leninist conviction and who are, therefore, able to subvert their egotism with regard to independent approaches to teaching.

CHAPTER VIII

POLYTECHNICAL EDUCATION
"RUECKT IN DAS LEBEN HINEIN"

Professor Dr. Heinz Frankiewicz is the director of the Institute for Mathematical, Scientific, and Polytechnical Instruction at the Academy of Pedagogical Sciences of the GDR and he is a leading architect of the GDR's contemporary approach to polytechnical education. His office at the academy is on the Otto Grotewohl Strasse near the corner of Unter Den Linden and, on an afternoon in August, 1977, I had the opportunity to discuss with him the socialist concept of polytechnical education and its current practice in the GDR. His considerable knowledge, which included not only technical areas but philosophy, history, and literature as well, for the purpose of emphasizing and illustrating points was impressive. The following is a narrative compilation of his contributions to our discussion.

Polytechnical education and training is an aspect of the total education of young people in the GDR and in other socialist countries. It is a condition for the realization of a humanist concept of education, a concept which, it should be noted, is different than what is generally considered to be a humanist education in the West. A humanist education in the Communist sense, that is, an all-around education, refers to the educational goal that all people, not only specific or privileged individuals, should be provided with the opportunity for maximum intellectual and physical development for the future benefit of society. The basis for this definition of humanist education is found in the work of Karl Marx. The problem, however, is to realize this ideal and make it operative in contemporary socialist society.

Philosophers have stated that this educational ideal, the Communist concept of a humanist education, is not realizable in presocialist society. Marx said that there is a contradiction between work and learning in bourgeois society. However, in order to achieve humanism in the Communist sense, social contradictions such as that which exists between mental and physical or manual labor, must be eliminated. In the GDR and other socialist societies, the school must achieve this. The school must work to eliminate the contradiction between mental and physical labor, to develop the potentialities of the students, and, at the same time, to prepare them for vocations. According to Marx, the humanitarian school must prepare students in all areas including the humanities and technical areas and this kind of education can only be provided by a polytechnical school.

A polytechnical school is defined as: (1) a school that is oriented towards the humanist concept of education, and (2) a school that has the important goal of preparing young people for future work. The word "preparation" as it is used here is to be understood in the sense that the contradiction between intellectual and physical activity is resolved and that young people are guided to develop the attitude that they are owners of their country and places of work even though this cannot yet be realized in fact. According to this definition of the polytechnical school, all subjects have the dual goal of developing humanist ideals in young people—the compound word *Menschenbildung* is used to describe this process in the GDR—and preparing them for future work activity. Polytechnical education is, therefore, a preparation for life.

Subjects taught in the ten-year general polytechnical secondary school are selected on the basis of the contribution they can make towards *Menschenbildung* and work preparation. Marx said that people change only to the extent that they are able to change their environment. For education this means that a school must be developed in which *Menschenbildung* or the development of humanist ideals is achieved while, at the same time, students learn to build a new society. In this connection it is important to realize that to educate young people without connecting learning to work is to provide them with an education conducive to the development of egotism and to prevent them from realizing that society will make requirements of them.

A problem in trying to realize polytechnical education in the GDR at the present time is that the specialization which characterizes industrial society does not require this kind of general education. For example, 60 percent of the young people currently completing vocational training are overqualified. This is a contradiction that the GDR must live with for the next fifteen to twenty years. The goal is to resolve this contradiction between general education and vocational training by raising the level of working requirements. Job requirements must be raised because the schools will not reduce their requirements.

In this regard, it is interesting to consider present science requirements in the polytechnical school. The educational program of the
ten-year general polytechnical secondary school delineates what is
required of basic education in socialist society today. With reference
to the science courses required by this program, we must ask on
what basis can a person relate to nature without a fundamental
knowledge of the natural sciences? For example, a whole range of
environmental factors cannot be understood without the study of
chemistry. The periodic system in nature cannot be understood
without understanding the periodic system in chemistry, the building of elements, and atomic structure. The role of chemistry becomes even clearer when we consider vocational activities and the
importance of chemistry in understanding aspects of modern life. A
broad understanding of technology is important for successful living
in modern industrial society, since a diversified technical knowledge
serves as a basis for coping with job displacement imposed by the
growth of technical society.

A continual effort is made in the ten-year general polytechnical
secondary school to relate theoretical learning, particularly in the
natural and social sciences, with the practical activity of the students.
A good illustration of learning by relating theory to practice can be
taken from the tenth-grade physics program in which students study
inductance and capacitance and, through working with coils and
capacitators, begin to develop an understanding of electromagnetic
waves. Approximately 25 percent of these student do their productive work in electrical industries where they have an opportunity to
see the practical application of these laws. Students who are working in
agricultural enterprises have the chance to experience the applications
of biological theories. Another example of learning by correlating
theory and practice can be taken from instruction in the field of economics. In economics classes, students learn the laws of economics
in the form of conflict-free theory, whereas in the factory environment they learn the contradictions involved in putting theory into
practice.

Stressing the humanities in general education is a different educational concept than that which is practiced in the socialist countries.
Of course, a person who is educated mainly in the humanities is well
prepared to understand the development of human beings, but it is
also important to acquire an understanding of the natural sciences
and technology. How will a person approach the end of this century,
for example, if they are educated only in the humanities and under-

stand nothing of the environment, of science and technology? Or how can young people come to terms with the pessimism of Jaspers and other existentialist writers without a solid technical education? (Commenius defined general education as one that provides the basis for understanding any essential aspect of the environment, not in all details, but in general. Goethe understood that people realize themselves only when they are active. Of course, Goethe could not foresee the forms of activity in industrial society. For him, the *Handwerker* or skilled craftsman was the universal man. Marx saw the industrial worker as the universal man, but only when the worker understands his role in relation to the entire spectrum of activity in his industry.

In the GDR, an effort is being made to balance education in the natural and social sciences. This approach to educating young people is more humanistic than that which concentrates heavily on the humanities; and it is a more valuable preparation for life. Polytechnical education seeks to make education relevant to life. *Es rueckt in das Leben hinein!*

CHAPTER IX

CONCLUSIONS

In assessing education in the socialist countries, it is not our intent to pass judgment on the underlying ideologic Marxist-Leninist basis of their government system. Rather, it is in the interest of the West to become familiar with the kind of education that young people in these countries are acquiring for the purpose of developing a more valid conception of their attitudes and, particularly, for the purpose of extracting those apolitical ideas and concepts that have a universal pedagogical validity and are of potential applicability within our own systems.

In the preceding pages, we have presented a tableau of the education of GDR youth in a social context. We have examined the philosophical basis of education in contemporary socialist society, the methodology of instruction, and the professional education and training of teachers. Our purpose has been to provide a description of a relatively inaccessible aspect of East German life, and the resulting insights serve as a basis for formulating certain broad statements regarding the education of young people in the GDR.

The purpose, emphasis, and scope of compulsory education and training is rooted in the philosophy of Marxism-Leninism which furnishes the economic and social foundation for the socialist society which has evolved in the GDR. The primary motivation of the GDR's Communist leadership is to develop the country's economic productivity within the framework of a maturely developed socialist society and in cooperation with the community of COMECON nations. A competitive posture is assumed by the GDR and all other Communist-led nations vis-à-vis the leading industrial nations of the West with the long-range economic objective of achieving an economic supremacy of Communist over non-Communist societies. The purpose of all aspects of GDR society, including education, is, therefore, to contribute to attaining this ultimate goal.

Young people in the GDR are educated according to a unified, mandatory plan that has been developed and continues to evolve on the basis of extensive pedagogical research and investigation. The task of compulsory education in the GDR and in the socialist countries, in general, is to prepare young people for life in a socialist society—a society that requires ideological conformity and increasing technological productivity. In the GDR, the educational program of the schools is designed to make effective contributions to both of these requirements.

The direct relation between increased economic productivity and continual technological development is reflected in the prominence of science and related subjects in the compulsory program of study of the general schools. Communist educators contend that a more intensive emphasis on education in science and mathematics, which includes a firm knowledge of theory as well as of the practical application of this theory in modern technological production, constitutes a base element for the further training of a technical labor force capable of filling current production norms and the ambitious economic aspirations of the GDR. Additionally, science education is considered to be a primary means of inculcating youth with Communist ideology and its related world view. Basic to this process is the interpretation of natural science from the Marxist-Leninist philosophical position and promulgation of the belief that Marxism-Leninism furnishes the only correct interpretation of reality.

The curriculum of the GDR's ten-year general polytechnical secondary school is so structured that the subject matter of any given course is integrated with the subject matter of other academic areas of study. The all-encompassing nature of the Marxist-Leninist ideological-philosophical system is a key unifying factor. In addition to the reinforcement value that a unified approach to learning has on the development of a unified world view, East German educators contend that a systematic presentation of diverse subject matter contributes effectively to an orderly intellectualization of the material presented and provides an essential framework for the further acquisition and retention of information.

Classroom instruction is a mixture of traditional methods such as teacher lecturing and demonstrations as well as classroom discussions which tend to consist of teacher-guided question-and-answer sessions. Science instruction is characterized by many student experiments that are richly integrated into the teaching process. Efforts are continually made to find more effective ways of presenting instructional material and more relevant topics for instruction.

An essential aspect of the contemporary approach to socialist compulsory education is the emphasis placed on learning fundamentals. Traditional learning methods, including memorization, are evoked for this purpose, since, according to GDR educators, experience has proven them to be most effective for building a solid foundation of factual and theoretical knowledge. Student attainment of learning objectives is tested according to a system of state-planned and regulated examinations given annually in all subjects at each grade level. These competency examinations have the dual function of regulating the quality of education being provided for young people and of reinforcing learning as a consequence of the recapitulation of subject matter required in preparing for them. Thus, those Western critics who, for ideological or other reasons, denigrate the achievements of socialist education and view it as having little substance apart from its propaganda content, are shortsighted. When we compare the compulsory education of East German youth with that required of young people in the United States, for example, we find that the GDR puts a heavier emphasis on mathematics, the sciences, and social studies. By the time they have completed ten years of compulsory education, all young people in the GDR have studied mathematics for ten years, physics for five years, chemistry for four years, and astronomy for one year. Requirements in the social studies of history, civics, and geography include instruction for periods of six, four, and six years, respectively.

In contrast, recent statistics compiled in the United States reveal that less than a year of study is required for high school graduation by 22 percent of the states in mathematics, 12 percent in science, and 2 percent in social studies; and, that only 21 percent of the states require more than a year of mathematics and science education, whereas 68 percent require more than a year of social studies.[1] According to this study, 15 percent of the states had "unknown" science requirements and 13 percent had "unknown" social studies requirements. Another report notes that, "for about 50 percent of the students, biology is their last science course, usually in grade 10."[2] Added to the fact that mathematics and science requirements in the United States are generally inadequate and reflect a lack of foresight in educational planning, the introduction of "innovative" teaching and learning methods has contributed to an erosion of the level of attainment of basic knowledge required by American compulsory education. A major aspect of the appeal of these methods to teachers as well as students is the promise that the tedium of learning can be replaced by a "making learning fun" approach. As recent studies indicate, however, such methods tend to be ineffective.[3] Furthermore, their utilization contributes to conditioning young people towards the accumulation of superficial information as a substitute for basic knowledge. This tendency towards superficiality, which is also seen as a reaction on the part of young people to the vast amounts of knowledge with which they are confronted in modern industrial society, is reduced in GDR youth through a uniform emphasis on basic learning.

The policy of centralizing education in the socialist countries has the advantages that (1) instructional goals can be set at the national level, (2) the most effective means for attaining these goals can be implemented, and (3) the quality of education can be controlled throughout the country. Inherent in the centralization of institutions, however, is a greater limitation of emphasis on the individual than is the case in the decentralized organization which typifies contemporary education in the United States, for example. Socialist compulsory education is a process by which the individual is prepared for living within the framework of socialist society and the controlled development of the individual is encouraged in those directions deemed most constructive for achieving centrally determined national goals.

The controlled development of the individual for the national good in socialist society has implications for individual creativity. A basic tenet underlying the approach to compulsory education in the GDR is that creativity should be founded on knowledge. The function of the school is to form this foundation of basic knowledge, rather than to cater to individual interest before a solid fundamental education has been achieved. A system of after-school activities has been developed for the latter purpose and creativity is encouraged within the framework of these activities. The creativity, however, is controlled in the sense that goal orientation imposes restrictions on it. For example, in the area of science and technology, an emphasis is put on the kind of creativity that will in some way contribute to the GDR's national economic development and its prestige. In general, the limitations imposed on creativity are defined by the policy decisions of the party leadership and determined by what it considers to be in its best interests.

Another aspect of the restrictions on self-expression required by socialist society concerns vocational opportunity. In most cases, decisions regarding vocations to be pursued in adult life are made by students during the secondary stage of compulsory education on the basis of available information concerning future national occupational requirements and the availability of corresponding training positions. Although individual interest is considered in the vocational decision-making process, the primary factor in career determination is national need. Students are expected to be capable of subordinating personal to national interests as a result of their acquired Marxist-Leninist conviction. Thus, it is not uncommon for young people to be trained for occupations in which they have little or no specific interest.

The planned restriction of vocational opportunity is a fundamental aspect of economic planning in socialist societies. The primary reason for imposing limitations on the vocational options available to young people is to provide an effective correspondence between the availability of trained workers and professionals and future job requirements. An advantage of such planning for young East Germans is that once they have completed their vocational or professional training, rather than being confronted with the potential of joblessness which is becoming an increasing problem for young people in the West, they have jobs waiting for them.

Currently, GDR youth are selected to attend the university-preparatory extended secondary schools in the eighth grade on the basis of demonstrated academic ability. Vocational decisions regarding young people who are not selected for university preparation, and this includes the majority of young East Germans, are generally made in the ninth grade. Although, theoretically, the possibility exists for changing vocational status at some later time, in practice, significant career changes are difficult to make and most young people in the GDR are "programmed" for vocational placement by the age of fifteen years.

A system that requires relatively permanent decisions regarding adult careers to be made on the basis of the intellectual development demonstrated by a child of fourteen or fifteen years of age lacks sufficient flexibility to accommodate the "late bloomer," i.e., the individual whose latent intellectual capabilities come to fruition after the age of fifteen years as a result of stimulated curiosity and interest and who, because of environmental conditions, did not have the benefit of intellectual stimulus and an emphasis on learning manifested in the home. By neglecting the role that interest and curiosity play in stimulating the intellectual capabilities of the late adolescent, the GDR is prevented from making maximum use of the reservoir of talent inherent in its youth.

Two consequences of this neglect for socialist society in the GDR are (1) the existence of an undercurrent of discontent with the status quo arising, in part, from the intellectual frustration caused by requiring individuals to spend a lifetime working at occupations that are beneath their level of intellectual capability and which do not conform to their interests and (2) the insufficient productive utilization of the creative potential of its citizens. At present, there is discussion in the GDR concerning the extension of the period of compulsory education to twelve years. If this plan is realized with a concomitant postponement of the age at which vocations are selected, some of the problems surrounding vocational decision-making may be ameliorated for young people in the GDR.

The most unique feature of contemporary socialist education is the polytechnical approach to learning which includes a program of polytechnical instruction. The relevancy that compulsory learning acquires through this approach is possibly socialist education's greatest achievement. School becomes part of the mainstream of life through the integration of theoretical learning with practical activity and productive work. Although it is based on the Marxist concept of the unity of theory and practice, the pedagogical potential of this method should not be overlooked in the West nor should it be lightly dismissed as a political fabrication of Marxism. Ideally, the polytechnical approach to educating young people facilitates their development of an educated familiarity with the environment and assists in the formation of realistic expectations about adult life through first-hand experiences in the adult world of daily work.

Considered *in toto*, the program for compulsory education in the GDR is impressive when looked at from the point of view of its historical development and within the framework of its major objective. This is to provide a basic foundation for the development of a socialistically conscious and technically capable labor force in a country that is critically short of mineral and fossil fuels and has limited land available for agricultural development and which must, therefore, export finished technology in order to survive economically.

The scope and depth of the overall program for compulsory education in the GDR also merits comment when considered in relation to extant programs for educating and training young people during the period of compulsory education in the United States and leading industrial nations of Western Europe. For example, in this regard it is interesting to note a recent comparison that has been made of the educational systems of the two Germanies, the GDR and the FRG, states that have had divergent political and socio-economic developments since their origin in the aftermath of World War II. According to this assessment which appeared in the West German press, the GDR's lead was conceded in the following terms:[4]

The lead can be measured. In the GDR, in proportion to the population, there are 70 percent more teachers than in the Federal Republic. Eighty-five percent of all pupils between the ages of fifteen and sixteen years complete an obligatory tenth year of school in the general polytechnical secondary school, the standard type school in the GDR (in the Federal Republic, this is still a long-range goal). Ninety-nine percent of all pupils matriculating from GDR schools learn a [profession or] vocation. In the Federal Republic, 10 percent remain without training.

The GDR invests more than 7 percent of its Gross National Product in education—a sum that is only a target for the 1980's in the Federal Republic (today it is 5 percent). Out of every one hundred inhabitants between the ages of eighteen and forty-five years, seventeen are attending technical colleges or universities (in the Federal Republic the number is fourteen); in 1972 there were a total of 390,000 students in the GDR, 110,000 more than in 1965.

Those who have jobs can study further. Approximately 168,000 GDR citizens are taking correspondence courses at training colleges or universities or attend evening courses. The statistics of success also make obvious the increasing equality of women: in 1972, more than half of all students in technical colleges and more than one-third of those in universities were women. In the Federal Republic approximately 25 percent of all students are women.

The earnestness with which educational policy is developed and put into practice today in the socialist countries underlines the weaknesses in our own approaches to compulsory education in the West. Contemporary systems of compulsory education in Western Europe and the United States are showing increasing signs of being incapable of preparing young people for effective and productive adult lives. They are failing to provide youth with an adequate basis for vocational education and training and are responsible for developing unrealistic goals and expectations concerning adult life. Young people in these countries are currently being described as "demoralized by joblessness." In contrast to the general approach to education in the West, which is all too often diffuse and lacking in a concrete sense of national direction or goals, the socialist countries, whatever may be our criticisms of the ideological fundament of their systems, appear to be striving to prepare their young people realistically. They are doing this through a polytechnical approach to compulsory education which seeks a balance between the vital areas of science and mathematics, on one hand, and the social sciences and humanities, on the other. Specifically, the GDR, fully aware of its precarious shortage of mineral and agricultural assets and the ideological conformity imposed on it by the Soviet Union, is making a determined effort to educate its young people to become viable members of a technological society with the goal of supporting the GDR's long-range ideologic and economic goals.

REFERENCES CITED

Introduction:

1. Peter Christian Ludz, *The German Democratic Republic from the Sixties to the Seventies: A Socio-Political Analysis* (Cambridge: Center for International Studies, Harvard University Press, 1970), p. 8.

2. IX. Party Congress of the SED, Berlin, 18-22 May 1976, *Programm der Sozialistischen Einheitspartei Deutschlands* (Berlin: Dietz Verlag, 1976), p. 73. (Hereafter referred to as SED.)

3. Eugene K. Keefe *et al., Area Handbook for East Germany* (Washington, D.C.: U.S. Government Printing Office, 1972), p. 165.

4. A. N. Yakovlev *et al., Fundamentals of Political Science* (Moscow: Progress Publishers, e975), p. 520.

5. GDR, Council of Ministers, The Ministry of Education, *Act on the Integrated Socialist Educational System of the German Democratic Republic* (Berlin: Staatsverlag der Deutschen Demokratischen Republik, 1972), p. 69. (Hereafter referred to as Act on ISES.)

Chapter I

1. George H. Sabine, *A History of Political Theory* (New York: Holt, Rinehart and Winston, 1961), pp. 884 and 922-24.

2. Robert Ulich, *The Education of Nations: A Comparison in Historical Perspective* (Cambridge: Harvard University Press, 1967),p.193.

3. David Childs, *East Germany* (New York: Frederick A. Praeger, 1969), p. 173.

4. A. N. Yakovlev *et al., Fundamentals of Political Science* (Moscow: Progress Publishers, 1975), p. 520.

5. Childs, p. 176.

6. Karl-Heinz Guenther and Gottfried Uhlig, *History of the Schools in the German Democratic Republic 1945 to 1968* (Berlin: Volk und Wissen Volkseigener Verlag, 1973), p. 18.

7. Mina J. Moore-Rinvolucri, *Education in East Germany* (Hamden, Connecticut: Archon Books, 1973), p. 19.

8. Arthur M. Hanhardt, Jr., *The German Democratic Republic* (Baltimore: The Johns Hopkins Press, 1968), p. 14.

9. Organisation for Economic Co-operation and Development, Education Committee, *Reviews of National Policies for Education: Germany* (Paris: Organisation for Economic Cooperation and Development, 1971), p. 3.

10. Jonathon Steele, *Inside East Germany: The State That Came in from the Cold* (New York: Urizen Books, Inc., 1977), p. 40.

11. Guenther and Uhlig, p. 21.

12. Ibid., p. 19.

13. Ibid., p. 28.

14. Gottfried Uhlig, *Dokumente zur Geschichte des Schulwesens in der Deutschen Demokratischen Republik, Teil 1: 1945-1955* (Berlin: Volk und Wissen Volkseigener Verlag, 1970), p. 179; and, Guenther and Uhlig, p. 26.

15. Guenther and Uhlig, p. 14.

16. Uhlig, p. 224.

17. Uhlig, p. 192; Guenther and Uhlig, p. 38; and, Karl-Heinz Guenther, *Dokumente zur Geschichte des Schulwesens in der Deutschen Demokratischen Republik, Teil 2: 1956-1967/8,* I (Berlin: Volk und Wissen Volkseigner Verlag, 1969), pp. 207-10.

18. Guenther and Uhlig, p. 42.

19. Moore-Rinvolucri, p. 24.

20. Childs, p. 176.

21. Guenther and Uhlig, p. 29.

22. Ibid, p. 29.

23. Ibid., pp. 28 and 30.

24. Smith, pp. 214-18.

25. Guenther and Uhlig, pp. 77-80.

26. Smith, p. 236.

27. Guenther and Uhlig, p. 76.

28. Guenther and Uhlig, p. 82.

29. Hanhardt, pp. 67-69.

30. Guenther and Uhlig, pp. 96-97.

31. Harmut Zimmermann, "The GDR in the 1970's," *Problems in Communism*, XXVII (March-April, 1978), p. 4.

32. Ibid., p. 9.

33. Kurt Gerhard Fischer, *Polytechnische Erziehung* (Goettingen: Vandenhoeck und Ruprecht, 1970), p. 104.

34. Guenther and Uhlig, pp. 131-32.

35. Ibid., pp. 163-64.

Chapter II

1. Gustav A. Wetter, *Dialectical Materialism* (New York: Frederick A. Praeger, 1958), p. 283.

2. V. I. Lenin, *Materialism and Empirio-Criticism* (New York: International Publishers, 1927), p. 128. (Hereafter referred to as ME.)

3. Wetter, p. 296.

4. Ibid., p. 298.

5. F. Engels, *Preparatory Writings for Anti-Duehring*, printed as an appendix to *Anti-Duehring* (Moscow: n.p., 1954), quoted in Wetter, p. 299.

6. F. Engels, *Dialectics of Nature* (Moscow: n.p., 1954), p. 328, quoted in Wetter, p. 300.

7. Engels, *Anti-Duehring*, p. 158, quoted in Wetter, p. 252.

8. F. V. Konstantinov and others, *Fundamentals of Marxist Philosophy* (Moscow: n.p., 1962), p. 196, cited in Richard T. DeGeorge, *Patterns of Soviet Thought* (Ann Arbor: The University of Michigan Press, 1966), p. 212.

9. Wetter, p. 320.

10. Konstantinov, p. 196, cited in DeGeorge, p. 212.

11. J. V. Stalin, *History of the Communist Party of the Soviet Union (Bolsheviks)* (Moscow: n.p., n.d.), p. 109, quoted in Wetter, p. 333.

12. Wetter, p. 338.

13. Ibid., p. 356.

14. Ibid., p. 356.

15. G. F. Alexandrov, ed., *Dialectical Materialism* (Moscow, n.p., 1954), p. 9, quoted in Wetter, p. 251.

16. DeGeorge, p. 52.

17. Wetter, p. 356.

18. Lenin, ME, p. 38.

19. Ibid., p. 44.

20. Lenin, cited in DeGeorge, p. 152.

21. Wetter, p. 499.

22. Lenin, cited in DeGeorge, p. 152.

23. Lenin, ME, p. 38.

24. Wetter, p. 499.

25. Lenin, ME, p. 99.

26. M. N. Rutkevich, *Praktika—osnova poznoniya i kriteriy istiny* (Practice as the Foundation of Knowledge and Criterion of Truth) (Moscow: n.p., 1952), p. 125, quoted in Wetter, p. 507.

27. F. V. Konstantinov and others, *The Fundamentals of Marxist-Leninist Philosophy* (Moscow: Progress Publishers, 1974), p. 545.

28. Rutkevich, cited in Wetter, pp. 507-08.

29. Rutkevich, op. cit., p. 142, quoted in Wetter, p. 513.

30. V. I. Lenin, *Aus dem philosophischen Nachlass. Exzerpte und Randglossen* (Berlin: n.p., 1949), p. 121, quoted in Wetter, p. 513.

31. Loc. cit.

32. Lenin, ME, p. 133.

33. DeGeorge, p. 155.

34. Engels, cited in Lenin, ME, p. 136.

35. Lenin, ME, pp. 106-07.

36, Sabine, p. 772.

37. Use of the word "science" by Marx and in Marxist-Leninist philosophy, in general, is closer in meaning to the ordinary English usage of the word "knowledge," when it is used accurately and objectively, rather than to the popular usage of the word "science" in the English language which refers to repeatable experiments made under strict controls. DeGeorge, p. 56.

38. Karl Marx and Friedrich Engels, "The Communist Manifesto (1848)," *Capital, The Communist Manifesto, and Other Writings by Karl Marx*, ed. Max Eastman (New York: The Modern Library, 1932), p. 321. (The book is hereafter referred to as CCM.)

39. Ibid., p. 328.

40. Karl Marx, *Capital* (New York: The Modern Library, n.d.), p. 190.

41. Karl Marx, "From the 'Criticism of The Gotha Program'," CCM, p. 355.

42. Friedrich Engels, cited in M. M. Bober, *Karl Marx's Interpretation of History* (Cambridge: Harvard University Press, 1962), p. 271.

43. Karl Marx, quoted in V. I. Lenin, *State and Revolution* (New York: International Publishers, 1943), p. 76.

44. DeGeorge, p. 72.

45. Karl Marx, quoted in Lenin, *State and Revolution*, p. 78.

46. Friedrich Engels, *Socialism, Utopian and Scientific* (New York: n.p., 1892), pp. 76-77, quoted in Bober, p. 275.

47. Karl Marx, *Capital*, p. 581, cited in Bober, loc. cit.

48. Karl Marx and Friedrich Engels, p. 336.

49. Sabine, p. 806.

50. V. I. Lenin, *What Is To Be Done?* (New York: International Publishers, 1929), p. 126, quoted in DeGeorge, p. 138; and Sabine, p. 815.

51. Sabine, p. 815.

52. Jane Degras (ed.), *The Communist International, 1919-1943*, I (London: n.p., 1956), p. 128, quoted in Sabine, p. 858.

53. Yakovlev, p. 125.

54. J. V. Stalin, "On the Problems of Leninism," *Problems of Leninism* (Moscow: n.p., 1940), p. 135, quoted in Sabine, p. 860.

55. Sabine, p. 880.

56. DeGeorge, p. 174.

57. Sabine, p. 856.

58. Friedrich Engels, *Dialectics of Nature* (Moscow: Progress Publishers, 1972), p. 8.

59. Loc. cit.

60. G. F. Alexandrov, ed., *Dialectical Materialism* (Moscow: n.p., 1954), p. 9, quoted in Wetter, p. 251.

61. Wetter, p. 251; M. A. Leonov, cited in Wetter, loc. cit.; and, V. Svetlov and T. Oyzerman, quoted in Wetter, loc. cit.

62. B. M. Kedrov, cited in Wetter, p. 250.

63. G. F. Alexandrov, *History of Western European Philosophy* (Moscow: n.p., 1946), quoted in Wetter, p. 252.

64. Leonov, quoted in Wetter, p. 252.

65. Engels, *Dialectics of Nature*, p. 6.

66. A. S. Milovidov and V. G. Kozlov, eds., *The Philosophical Heritage of V. I. Lenin and Problems of Contemporary War* (Moscow: Military Publishing House, Voyenizdat, 1972), translated and published under the auspices of the United States Air Force, U.S. Government Printing Office, Washington, D.C., p. 174.

67. Loc. cit.

68. Ibid., p. 173.

69. Lenin, quoted in Milovidov, p. 174.

70. Milovidov, p. 174.

71. Loc. cit.

72. DeGeorge, p. 224, also see Wetter, p. 561.

73. DeGeorge, p. 234.

74. Konstantinov, cited in DeGeorge, p. 217.

75. "The New Communist Manifesto," *The New Communist Manifesto and Related Documents*, ed. Dan N. Jacobs (New York: Harper Torchbooks/The Academy Library, 1965), p. 21.

76. Konstantinov, cited in DeGeorge, p. 217.

77. DeGeorge, pp. 217 and 236.

78. Konstantinov, cited in DeGeorge, p. 218.

79. DeGeorge, p. 227.

80. Ibid., p. 229.

81. Yakovlev, pp. 287 and 291.

82. "The New Communist Manifesto," p. 34.

83. Loc. cit.

84. Margot Honecker, "Der gesellschaftliche Auftrag unserer Schule," *VIII. Paedagogischer Kongress der DDR 1978: Protokoll* (Berlin: Volk und Wissen Volkseigener Verlag, 1979), p. 81.

Chapter III

1. Act on ISES, p. 10.

2. Ibid., p. 15.

3. *Education for Today and Tomorrow* (Dresden: Verlag Zeit im Bild, 1973), p. 23.

4. *World Survey of Education,* Vol. IV, *Educational Policy, Legislation, and Administration* (Paris: UNESCO, 1971), p. 518.

5. Act on ISES, p. 37.

6. *World Survey of Education*, Vol. V, p. 520.

7. Helmut Klein, *First Hand Information: Education in a Socialist Country* (Dresden: Grafischer Grossbetrieb Voelkerfreundschaft, 1976), p. 51.

8. Ludz, p. 17.

9. *Statistisches Jahrbuch der Deutschen Demokratischen Republik* (Berlin: Staatsverlag der Deutschen Demokratischen Republik, 1976), p. xviii. (Hereafter referred to as SJ).

10. Act on ISES, p. 21.

11. Interview with Sigfried Bollmann, Director of the Department of International Relations, Ministry of Education of the GDR on November 11, 1975.

12. SJ, pp. 328-31.

13. Loc. cit.; and information from reliable GDR sources.

14. SJ, pp. 328-32.

15. Kurt Haspas, *Methodik des Physikunterrichts* (Berlin: Volk und Wissen Volkseigener Verlag, 1974), p. 21.

16. Loc. cit.

17. Thirty-fifth Session of the International Conference on Public Education, Geneva, 1975, *Development of Public Education in the German Democratic Republic* (Berlin: Ministry of Education, 1975), p. 37.

18. Engels, *Dialectics of Nature*, p. 170.

19. SED, p. 48.

20. Cf., p. 2-22.

21. Deborin, cited in Wetter, p. 162.

22. *Education for Today and Tomorrow*, p. 28.

23. Haspas, p. 28.

24. Herman Ley and Karl-Friedrich Wessel and others, *Weltanschaulich-philosophische Bildung und Erziehung im mathematischen und naturwissenschaftlichen Unterricht (Beitraege)* (Berlin: Volk und Wissen Volkseigener Verlag, 1974), pp. 44-111.

25. Lenin, quoted in Milovidov, p. 175.

26. Bernal, quoted in Heinz Frankiewics, *Technik und Bildung in der Schule der DDR* (Berlin: Volk und Wissen Volkseigener Verlag, 1968), p. 57. (Hereafter referred to as TB.)

27. Frankiewicz, TB, pp. 108-11;

28. Ibid., pp. 55-56.

Chapter IV

1. Engels, *Dialectics of Nature*, p. 170.

2. Karl Marx, *Capital* (New York: The Modern Library, n.d.), pp. 533-34.

3.. Heinz Frankiewicz and others, *Paedagogische Enzyklopedie*, II (Berlin: VEB Deutscher Verlag der Wissenschaften, 1963), p. 729. (Hereafter referred to as PE II.); and, Marx and Engels, *Concerning Education and Training* (Berlin: n.p., 1961), quoted in Frankiewicz, PE II, p. 731.

4. Nadezhda Krupskaya, cited in Kenneth F. Smart, "The Polytechnical Principle," *Communist Education*, ed. Edmund J. King (London: Methuen and Co., Ltd., 1963), p. 156.

5. *Neues Deutschland*, January 17, 1979.

6. Klaus-Dieter Mende, *Die Polytechnische Erziehung im Schulsystem der DDR* (Bad Harzburg: Verlag fuer Wissenschaft, Wirtschaft, und Technik, 1972), p. 34.

7. Frankiewicz, TB, pp. 50-53.

8. Loc. cit.

9. Erwin Kohn and Fred Postler, *Polytechnical Education in the GDR* (Dresden: Verlag Zeit im Bild, 1973), p. 15.

10. Heinz Frankiewicz, "Polytechnische Bildung und Erziehung und Verbindung von Unterricht und produktiver Arbeit in der allgemeinbildenden polytechnischen Oberschule der DDR," *VII. Internationales Paedagogisches Kolloquium* (Berlin: Ministerium fuer Volksbildung und UNESCO-Kommission der Deutschen Demokratischen Republik, 1976), p. 71. (Hereafter referred to as VII IPK.)

11. Ibid, pp. 73-74.

12. Ibid., p. 73.

13. Loc. cit.

14. Kohn and Postler, p. 167.

15. Smart, p. 167.

16. Kohn and Postler, p. 41.

17. Ibid., pp. 36-40; and, Gerhart Neuner and others, *Allgemein-bildung Lehrplanwerk Unterricht* (Berlin: Volk und Wissen Verlag, 1973), p. 227.

18. Frankiewicz, VII IPK, p. 76.

19. Kohn and Postler, p. 41.

20. Frankiewicz, VII IPK, p. 78.

21. Kohn and Postler, p. 41.

22. Frankiewicz, VII IPK, p. 80.

23. Ibid., p. 81.

Chapter V

1. Act on ISES, p. 37.

2. Statement made by S. Bollmann during a meeting at the Ministry of Education in Berlin on March 11, 1977.

3. Guenther and Uhlig, p. 161.

4. Ibid., p. 162.

5. 35th Session . . . , *Development of Public Education in GDR*, p. 12.

6. Guenther and Uhlig, p. 174.

7. Ibid., pp. 174-75.

8. Statement made by Eberhard Rossa, Deputy Director, Department of Natural Sciences, Academy of Pedagogical Sciences of the German Democratic Republic, November 3, 1976.

9. Loc. cit.

10. Haspas, p. 96.

11. Konstantinov, p. 545.

12. Loc. cit.

13. Konstantinov, pp. 545-46.

14. Ibid., pp. 546-47.

15. Ibid., p. 541.

16. Ibid., p. 546.

17. Urie Bronfenbrenner, "Theory and Research in Soviet Character Education," *Social Thought in the Soviet Union*, ed. Alex Simirenko (Chicago: Quadrangle Books, 1969), p. 279.

18. Haspas, p. 73.

19. Margot Honecker, ¨*Wir Lehren und lernen im Geiste Lenins,*¨ *DIZ Information.* 20/21 (1970), p. 32.

20. Loc. cit.

21. Honecker, ". . . *im Geiste Lenins*," p. 33.

22. Loc. cit.

23. Honecker, ". . . *im Geiste Lenins*," p. 33; and, Neuner, p. 499.

24. Neuner, p. 514.

25. Eberhard Rossa and others, *Methodik Chemieunterricht* (Berlin: Volk und Wissen Volkseigener Verlag, 1975), p. 165.

26. Ibid., p. 167.

27. Neuner, p. 499; and, Rossa, pp. 176-77.

28. Rossa, pp. 176-77.

29. Rossa, pp. 178-80; and, Neuner, p. 499.

30. Rossa, pp. 180-87.

31. Margot Honecker, *"Inhaltliche Ausgestaltung der Oberschule— Programm unserer weiteren Arbeit," Protokoll der zentralen Direktorenkonferenz des Ministeriums fuer Volksbildung*, May 8 and 9, 1973, quoted in Rossa, p. 181.

32. Neuner, p. 111.

33. Rossa, pp. 188-91; and, Neuner, p. 500.

34. Neuner, p. 500.

35. Haspas, pp. 102-07; and, Rossa, pp. 165-69.

36. Rossa, pp. 169-75.

37. Ibid., p. 172.

38. Neuner, p. 192.

39. Rossa, pp. 193, 195, and 197.

40. Ibid., p. 207.

41. Ibid., pp. 207-08.

42. Honecker, ". . . *im Geiste Lenins*," p. 33.

43. Loc. cit.

44. Loc. cit.

45. Statement made by Eberhard Rossa during interview of November 3, 1976.

46. The material for this section is based upon statements made by Eberhard Rossa during the interview of November 3, 1976.

47. Honecker, "Der gesellschaftliche Auftrag unserer Schule," p. 107.

48. Ibid., p. 108.

Chapter VI

1. Honecker, "Der gesellschaftliche Auftrag unserer Schule," p. 116.

2. Act ISES, p. 39.

3. Siegfried Baer and Rudi Slomma, *Lehrerausbildung und Lehrerweiterbildung in der DDR* (Berlin: Ministerium fuer Volksbildung in der DDR und der UNESCO-Kommission der DDR, 1973), pp. 15-19.

4. Ibid., p. 23; and, statement by S. Bollmann during meeting of March 11, 1977.

5. Baer and Slomma, pp. 28-29.

6. Ibid., p. 28.

7. *Lehrprogramme fuer die Ausbildung von Diplomlehrern der allgemeinbildenden polytechnischen Oberschulen im Fach Physik* (Berlin: Ministerium fuer Volksbildung, 1975), p. 82.

8. Baer and Slomma, pp. 28-31.

9. Ibid., p. 31.

10. Ibid., p. 32.

11. Ibid., p. 33.

12. Loc. cit.

13. Loc. cit.

14. Baer and Slomma, p. 34.

15. Loc. cit.

16. Baer and Slomma, p. 35.

17. Loc. cit.

18. Baer and Slomma, p. 36.

19. Loc. cit.

20. Ibid., p. 37.

21. Ibid., p. 38.

22. *Lehrprogramme fuer die Ausbildung von Diplomlehrern der allgemeinbildenden polytechnischen Oberschulen im Fach Biologie* (Berlin: Minstry of Education, 1976), p. 118.

23. Ibid., p. 119.

24. *Lehrprogramme . . . im Fach Physik*, pp. 80-81; and, Baer and Slomma, p. 27.

25. *Lehrprogramm fuer die Ausbildung von Diplomlehrern der allgemeinbildenden polytechnischen Oberschulen in Methodik des Biologie-unterrichts* (Berlin: Ministry of Education, 1976), p. 54.

26. Baer and Slomma, p. 41.

27. Hans-Joachim Giersber, Hartmut Knitter, and Hans Hoffmann, *Potsdam and Sans Souci* (Dresden: Verlag Zeit im Bild, 1975), pp. 7 and 16-18.

28. Baer and Slomma, pp. 29-30; and, *Lehrprogramme . . . Fach Physik*, p. 80.

29. *Lehrprogramme fuer die Ausbildung von Diplomlehrern der allgemeinbildenden polytechnicschen Oberschule im Fach Chemie* (Berlin: Ministry of Education, 1975), pp. 72-75; *Lehrprogramme. . . Fach Physik*, pp. 62-65; and, *Lehrprogramme . . . Fach Biologie*, pp. 100-07.

Chapter VII

1. Statement made by S. Bollmann during a meeting at the Ministry of Education in Berlin on March 11, 1977.

2. Wolfgang Manthei, *Physik 10 Praktikum* (Berlin: Volk und Wissen Volkseigener Verlag, 1974).

3. SJ, pp. 1 and 2.

4. Statements made and information given by Eberhard Rossa during the interview in Berlin on November 3, 1976.

5. Haspas, pp. 87-89.

Chapter IX

1. Iris R. Weiss, *Report of the 1977 National Survey of Science, Mathematics, and Social Studies Education* (North Carolina: Center for Educational Research and Evaluation, 1978), p. 24.

2. Stanley L. Helgeson, Patricia E. Blosser, and Robert W. Howe, *The Status of Pre-College Science, Mathematics, and Social Science Education: 1955-1975; Volume 1: Science Education* (Columbus, Ohio: Center for Science and Mathematics Education, The Ohio State University, 1977), pp. 24-26.

3. "U.S. Lapsing into Illiteracy, Expert Claims," *The Stars and Stripes*, February 15, 1979.

4. *"Bald ein armes Volk von Professoren?"* Der Spiegel, April 22, 1974.

BIBLIOGRAPHY

MARXIST-LENINIST THEORY

Bober, M. M. *Karl Marx's Interpretation of History*. Cambridge: Harvard University Press, 1962.

DeGeorge, Richard T. *Patterns of Soviet Thought*. Ann Arbor: The University of Michigan Press, 1966.

    The development of Marxist-Leninist philosophy is traced through the process of summarizing the works of major and minor philosophers from Marx to contemporary theoreticians. A detail-critique of their important ideas is presented.

Eastman, Max. (ed.). *Capital, The Communist Manifesto, and Other Writings by Karl Marx*. New York: The Modern Library, 1932.

Engels, Frederick. *Dialectics of Nature*. Moscow: Progress Publishers, 1972.

Hoerz, Herbert. *Marxistische Philosophie und Naturwissenschaften*. Berlin: Akademie-Verlag, 1976.

Jacobs, Dan N. (ed.). *The New Communist Manifesto and Related Documents*. New York: Harper Torchbooks/The Academy Library, 1965.

King, Edmund J. (ed.). *Communist Education*. London: Methuen and Co., Ltd., 1963.

Konstantinov, F. V. and others. *The Fundamentals of Marxist-Leninist Philosophy*. Moscow: Progress Publishers, 1974.

    This book deals systematically with the major problems of dialectical and historical materialism and has been thoroughly revised on the basis of experience and discussion and brought up-to-date with materials from the 24th Congress of the Communist Party of the Soviet Union.

Lenin, V. I. *Materialism and Empirio-Criticism*. New York: International Publishers, 1927.

    A major source of Marxist-Leninist philosophy, it was written in 1908 and is Lenin's fullest exposition of his position on the theory of knowledge and reality.

Lenin, V. I. *State and Revolution*. New York: International Publishers, 1943.

    A statement of Lenin's theory of revolution and his ideas concerning the state.

Marx, Karl. *Capital*. New York: The Modern Library, n.d.

The fundamental document in the exposition of Communist theory.

Marx, Karl and Friedrich Engels. *Ueber Paedagogik und Bildungs-Politik*. Berlin: Volk und Wissen Volkseigener Verlag, 1976.

Marx, Karl, Friedrich Engels, and V. I. Lenin. *On Historical Materialism: A Collection*. Moscow: Progress Publishers, 1972.

Milovidov, A. S. and Kozlov, V. G. (eds.). *The Philosophical Heritage of V. I. Lenin and Problems of Contemporary War*. Moscow: Military Publishing House, Voyenizdat, 1972. Translated and published under the auspices of the United States Air Force, U. S. Government Printing Office, Washington, D.C.

Sabine, George H. *A History of Political Theory*. New York: Holt, Rinehart and Winston, 1961.

A standard authoritative work on the interpretation of political theory.

Simirenko, Alex (ed.). *Social Thought in the Soviet Union*. Chicago: Quadrangle Books, 1969.

Wetter, Gustav A. *Dialectical Materialism; a Historical and Systematic Survey of Philosophy in the Soviet Union*, trans. Peter Heath. New York: Frederick A. Praeger, 1958.

A source book; generally considered to be a basic work in the interpretation of dialectical materialism.

Yakovlev, A. N. and others. *Fundamentals of Political Science*. Moscow: Progress Publishers, 1975.

An outline of the Marxist concept of society, factors in its development, and the social activity of the people.

Zarodov, K. *Leninism and Contemporary Problems of the Transition from Capitalism to Socialism*. Moscow: Progress Publishers, 1976.

THE GERMAN DEMOCRATIC REPUBLIC

General

Childs, David. *East Germany*. New York: Frederick A. Praeger, 1969.

Dornberg, John. *The Other Germany*. Garden City, New York: Doubleday Company, 1968.

Giersber, Hans-Joachim, Hartmut Knitter, and Hans Hollmann. *Potsdam and Sans Souci*. Dresden: Verlag Zeit im Bild, 1975.

Gleitze, Bruno, Peter Ludz, and others. *Die DDR nach 25 Jahren*. Berlin: Duncker und Humblot, 1975.

Hangen, Welles. *The Muted Revolution: East Germany's Challenge to Russia and the West*. New York: Alfred A. Knopf, 1966.

Hanhardt, Arthur M., Jr. *The German Democratic Republic*. Baltimore: The Johns Hopkins Press, 1968.

Holm, Hans Axel. *The Other Germans: Report from an East German Town*. Translated by Thomas Teal. New York: Pantheon Books, a division of Random House, Inc., 1970.

148   THE CHALLENGE OF COMMUNIST EDUCATION

Keefe, Eugene K. and others. *Area Handbook for East Germany*. Washington, D.C.: U.S. Government Printing Office, 1972.

Legters, Lyman Howard (ed.). *The German Democratic Republic: A Developed Socialist Society*. Boulder, Colorado: Westview Press, 1978.

Livingston, Robert Gerald. "East Germany Between Moscow and Bonn." *Foreign Affairs*, (January, 1972).

Ludz, Peter C. "Discovery and 'Recognition' of East Germany." *Comparative Politics*, II (July, 1970), 681-92.

Ludz, Peter Christian. *The German Democratic Republic from the Sixties to the Seventies: A Socio-Political Analysis*. Cambridge: Center for International Studies, Harvard University Press, 1970.

Smith, Jean Edward. *Germany Beyond the Wall*. Boston: Little, Brown and Company, 1969.

State Central Adminstration for Statistics. *Statistical Pocket Book of the German Democratic Republic 1975*. Berlin: Staatsverlag der Deutschen Demokratischen Republik, 1975.

Staatisches Jahrbuch der Deutschen Demokratischen Republik, Berlin: Staatsverlag der Deutschen Demokratischen Republik, 1975, 1976.

Steele, Jonathan. *Inside East Germany: The State that Came in from the Cold*. New York: Urizen Books, Inc., 1977.

Zimmerman, Harmut. "The GDR in the 1970's." *Problems in Communism*, XXVII (March-April, 1978), 1-40.

IX Party Congress of the SED, Berlin, May 18-22, 1976, *Programm der Sozialistischen Einheitspartei Deutschlands*. Berlin: Dietz Verlag, 1976.

Education

Baer, Siegfried and Slomma, Rudi. *Lehrerausbildung and Lehrerweiterbildung in der DDR*. Berlin: Ministerium fuer Volksbildung der DDR und der UNESCO-Kommission der DDR, 1973.

"Bald ein armes Volk von Professoren?" *Der Spiegel*, April 22, 1974, pp. 38-50.

Bibliographie der Paedagogischen Veroeffentlichungen in der DDR. Leipzig: Bibliographisches Institut, 1973.

Education for Today and Tomorrow. Dresden: Verlag Zeit im Bild, 1973.

Frankiewicz, Heinz. "Polytechnische Bildung und Erziehung und die Verbundung von Unterricht und produktiver Arbeit in der allgemeinbildenden polytechnischen Oberschule der DDR." *VII. Internationales Paedagogisches Kolloquium*, Berlin: Ministerium fuer Volksbildung und UNESCO-Kommission der Deutschen Demokratischen Republik, 1976.

Frankiewicz, Heinz. *Technik und Bildung in der Schule der DDR*. Berlin: Volk und Wissen Volkseigener Verlag, 1968.

GDR, Council of Ministers, The Ministry of Education. *Act on the Integrated Socialist Educational System of the German Democratic Republic.* Berlin: Staatsverlag der Deutschen Demokratischen Republik, 1972.

Guenther, Karl-Heinz. *Dokumente zur Geschichte des Schulwesens in der Deutschen Demokratischen Republik, Teil 2: 1956-1967/8.* I, II. Berlin: Volk und Wissen Volkseigener Verlag, 1969.

Guenther, Karl-Heinz and Uhlig, Gottfried. History of the Schools in the German Democratic Republic 1945-68. Berlin: Volk und Wissen Volkseigener Verlag, 1973.

Haspas, Kurt. *Methodik des Physikunterrichts.* Berlin: Volk und Wissen Volkseigener Verlag, 1974.

The authoritative work on physics education in the ten-year general polytechnic secondary school.

Honecker, Margot. "Der gesellschaftliche Auftrag unserer Schule." *VIII. Paedagogischer Kongress der DDR 1978: Protokoll.* Berlin: Volk und Wissen Volkseigener Verlag, 1979.

Speech delivered by Margot Honecker, Member of the Central Committee of the SED and Minister of Education, at the Eighth Educational Congress of the GDR.

Honecker, Margot. "Wir leben und lernen im Geiste Lenins." DLZ Information, 20/21 (1970), 19-48.

Kienitz, Werner, ed. *Einheitlichkeit und Differenzierung im Bildungswesen.* Berlin: Volk und Wissen Volkseigener Verlag, 1971.

An international comparison written by an author collective.

Klein, Helmut. *First Hand Information: Education in a Socialist Country.* Dresden: Verlag Zeit im Bild, 1973.

Klein, Margrete Siebert. "Science Instruction in East Germany: Where Education Meets Ideology." *The Science Teacher,* volume 45, number 9 (December, 1978), 24-28;

Kohn, Erwin and Postler, Fred. *Polytechnical Education in the GDR.* Dresden: Verlag Zeit im Bild, 1973.

Lange, Wilfried. *Gestaltung und Fuehrung des Polytechnischen Unterrichts.* Berlin: Volk und Wissen Volkseigener Verlag, 1972.

Ley, Hermann and Wessel, Karl-Friedrich and others. *Weltanschaulich-Philosophie Bildung und Erziehung im mathematischen und naturwissenschaftlichen Unterricht (Beitraege).* Berlin: Volk und Wissen Volkseigener Verlag, 1974.

The authoritative work on the interrelation of natural science and mathematics education and Marxist-Leninist ideology in the ten-yar general polytechnical secondary school.

Mende, Klaus-Dieter. *Die Polytechnische Erziehung im Schulsystem der DDR.* Bad Harzburg: Verlag fuer Wissenschaft, Wirtschaft, und Technik, 1972.

A brief history of the development of polytechnical education in the GDR. The text is supported with documents which are appended.

Moore-Rinvolucri, Mina J. *Education in East Germany*. Hamden, Connecticut: Archon Books, 1973.

Neuner, Gerhart. *Zur Theorie der sozialistischen Allgemeinbildung*. Berlin: Volk und Wissen Volkseigener Verlag, 1975.

Neuner, Gerhart and others. *Allgemeinbildung Lehrplanwek Unterricht*. Berlin: Volk und Wissen Volkseigener Verlag, 1973.
    An authoritative work on the ten-year general polytechnical secondary school.

Neuner, Gerhart, and others. *Erziehung sozialistischer Persoenlichkeiten: Erfahrungen und Erkenntnisse der II. Konferenz der Paedagogen sozialistischer Laender*. Berlin: Volk und Wissen Volkseigener Verlag, 1976.

Smart, Kenneth F. "The Polytechnical Principle." *Communist Education*. ed. Edmund J. King. London: Methuen and Co., Ltd., 1965.

Uhlig, Gottfried. *Dokumente zur Geschichte des Schulwesens in der Deutschen Demokratischen Republik. Teil 1: 1945-55*. Berlin: Volk und Wissen Volkseigener Verlag, 1970.

World Survey of Education, Vol. V, *Educational Policy, Legislation, and Administration*. Paris: UNESCO, 1971.

35th Session of the International Conference on Public Education, Geneva, 1975. *Development of Public Education in the German Democratic Republic*. Berlin: Ministry of Education of the GDR, 1975.

Periodicals

Paedagogik. The journal of the Academy of Pedagogical Sciences of the GDR, published monthly. Berlin: Volk und Wissen Volkseigener Verlag.

Polytechnische Bildung und Erziehung. Berlin: Volk und Wissen Volkseigener Verlag.

Vergleichende Paedagogik. Berlin: Volk und Wissen Volkseigener Verlag.

APPENDIX A

Act on the Integrated Socialist Educational System of the German Democratic Republic:

Part Four, Section I,
The Ten-Year General Polytechnical Secondary School

Article 13

(1) The ten-year general polytechnical secondary school— hereinafter called secondary school—is the fundamental type of school in the integrated socialist educational system.

(2) The secondary school imparts a modern, socialist general education as the foundation of any further education and of professional activity. Education in the secondary school is closely connected to life, to work, and to the activities of socialist construction. The secondary school brings up young people to be conscious socialist men and women taking an active part in the life of society.

(3) The secondary school is organized as an organic entity which guarantees a continuous process of education from the first to the tenth form. It is subdivided into
— the primary stage with forms one to three,
— the intermediate stage with forms four to six,
— the secondary stage with forms seven to ten.

Article 14

(1) The systematic education of the children begins at the *primary stage*. Fundamental skills in reading, writing and mathematics shall be developed for they constitute the basis of all further education. The pupils shall be made acquainted with their social environment, especially with their immediate locality, in a vivid and comprehensible way. They acquire the first knowledge and understanding or nature, work, and socialist society. During the whole process of education at the primary stage the children are brought up to love their socialist home country. The pupils shall get accustomed to fulfilling adequate duties gladly and conscientiously, to behave well in public, and to learn and work diligently and conscientiously. Lessons shall be closely connected with socially useful work.

(2) Instruction at the primary stage has the following main content:

- In German the abilities and skills in reading, writing and linguistic expression shall be systematically developed. First insights into the structure of their mother tongue shall be given. Proceeding from their local environment the children shall be made acquainted with objects and phenomena in nature and society.
- In mathematics the basic skills in calculating with natural numbers shall be developed in close connection with the training in abstracting and thinking. The children get to know simple mathematical relations and laws, and shall be enabled to formulate mathematical statements in sentences.
- In shop and manual crafts training and gardening at the primary stage elementary technical, technological and economic knowledge shall be imparted, and simple technical-constructive abilities and working skills developed. The pupils are provided with an initial survey of the economy in their local region.
- In the art subjects the children shall be instructed in singing, performing music, drawing, painting, and modelling. They shall acquire abilities to do creative work and to appreciate works of art. The children's joy in artistic activities shall be promoted.
- The physical training is centered upon an all-around physical education. By means of many different exercises and games, such characteristics as strength, courage, dexterity, perseverance, and speed shall be developed, leading to simple skills in sport. The children shall become accustomed to discipline, correct hygienic behavior, and regular physical activities in their leisure time.

Article 15

(1) At the *intermediate stage* specialized instruction in natural, and social sciences and in a foreign language begins. The basic skills learned at the primary stage shall be increasingly used as a means of acquiring knowledge. In conformity with the higher degree of physical and intellectual maturity the children shall be made acquainted in a more detailed way with the life of society, with work, science, technology, and culture. The scientific content and method of instruction, the increased social activity of the pupils, their participation in productive work, the attitudes and opinions already forming in the political and moral fields, which are significant for the further development of a socialist attitude to work. The pupils shall be enabled to run their social life in class and school collectives, in school clubs, and in the 'Ernst Thaelmann" pioneer organization more and more independently.

(2) Instruction at the intermediate stage has the following main content:

- In German the systematic courses in grammar and orthography shall be continued. They shall impart stable knowledge of grammar and orthography. The children's ability to express themselves in the language shall be further improved. The pupils shall be introduced to literature and accustomed to reading works of literature by themselves.

- In mathematics a confident command of basic mathematical ways of solving problems, the work with rules of arithmetic, the drawing of logical conclusions, and the introduction to some special mathematical methods of work shall be the primary aspects. It shall be guaranteed that the pupils learn how to apply their mathematical knowledge and skills in solving suitable problems, particularly in the natural sciences and in practical life.

- The aim of natural science is to make the pupils understand the laws in nature and their effectiveness as well as important principles and possibilities of utilizing them. Theoretically substantiated scientific experiments, tasks comprising observations and investigations, and excursions shall be carried out.

- In shop and manual crafts training and gardening simple technical, agro-biological and economic knowledge shall be imparted and the ability to think on lines of economy developed. Technical thinking shall be promoted; technical and technological facts shall be increasingly permeated by mathematics and natural science. Basic working skills shall be improved.

- Historical and political knowledge shall be imparted in the social sciences. The pupils shall learn to understand the laws that govern social development, and be taught to do their own thinking. Questions that arise in connection with the politico-ideological development of the pupils at the intermediate stage and concern current political events shall be dealt with in all school subjects, particularly in social science lessons, and answered comprehensively and convincingly, according to the pupil's age.

- Russian begins at the intermediate stage. The active command of the language is the main aspect. Abilities and skills in reading and writing shall be developed.

- Art education is mainly concerned with diverse activities and with the continuous improvement of the pupils' activities and skills in singing, performing music, drawing, painting, and modelling. The occupation with art serves the aim of developing the faculty of cognition and the power to experience rich feelings and imagination.

- In physical training basic instruction begun at the primary stage shall be continued. Special attention shall be paid to controlling

the body and keeping it healthy and fit by various sports activit-
ities. The physical education syllabus at this stage includes also a
systematic training in swimming. The pupils shall be enabled to
perform physical exercises in an exact way. Athletic competitions
shall be carried out more than before. Extracurricular sports activities shall cater for differentiated interests in this field.

(3) At the intermediate stage job information begins which takes
the pupils' state of development into account. They are made acquainted with the most important vocations within their area and within
the national economy—this is a precondition for a free choice of vocations at a later date, according to personal and social interests. It is
particularly important to orient the girls to technical and agricultural
vocations. This careers' guidance shall also enlist parents' support.

Article 16

(1) At the *secondary stage* secondary education is completed. It
creates the foundations of practical activities, of a responsible decision
concerning the choice of vocation, and of further vocational and scientific education and training. At the secondary stage general education
and vociationally oriented education are combined. All subjects are
taught by specialized teachers. Content and structure of the lessons
shall be oriented on the relevant sciences as far as possible. The pupils
shall be enabled more and more to understand and apply laws and
scientific theories. Their abilities shall be developed in such a way
that they master the fundamental technique of intellectual work and
that they can extend and consolidate their knowledge and skills on
their own.

(2) Instruction at the secondary stage has the following main
content:
  —In mathematics the pupils are introduced to analysis. Geometry
    and comprehensive mathematical relations are dealt with. Special
    attention shall be paid to mathematical deduction and logical
    argumentation. In accordance with the general trend of the
    mathematical penetration of sciences the pupils shall be enabled
    to apply mathematical knowledge and methods in other subjects,
    in their vocational training, and in practical life.
  —Natural science comprises physics, astronomy, chemistry, biology,
    and physical geography. In each subject a system of fundamental
    scientific facts, laws, methods, and processes is imparted to the
    pupils.
    Natural science lessons shall give an insight into the future tasks
    of natural science and its role as a direct productive force. Above
    all, the pupils shall be given a deep theoretical understanding of

the law-governed causes of phenomena and processes in nature. Natural processes are observed and natural science experiments prepared, carried out, and assessed in close connection with theoretical considerations and generalizations. This instruction shall impart a scientific concept of animate and inanimate nature to the pupils.

— Polytechnical instruction is intended systematically to familiarize the pupils with the scientific-technical, technological, and politico-economic foundations of socialist production. Practical activities shall be oriented more to operating the modern machines and equipment. Polytechnical training takes place in socialist enterprises. In forms nine and ten the pupils are given polytechnical instruction preparing them for a vocation, or a basic vocational training. Through close contacts between pupils and collective groups of working people, and through their independent and responsible execution of production tasks the pupils' socialist attitude to work shall be developed in a special degree.

— In social science lessons the pupils acquire fundamental historical and political knowledge. They come to understand the laws of social development, and are enabled to apply their knowledge of history and politics to current problems. Instruction in civics imparts fundamental economic, philosophical, and political knowledge in close connection with life, thus introducing the pupils to Marxism-Leninism. The pupils shall be led to recognize the historic role and national duty of the German Democratic Republic. They shall come to the conclusion that the future belongs to socialism in the whole of Germany. In accordance with their needs and interests the pupils shall participate in the intellectual and cultural life.

— In German, oral and written expression shall be further improved. This task, especially the development of the ability to express themselves and to write down facts in good German, is a principle in each subject. In literature the pupils shall be made acquainted with humanistic works of the past and present. The pupils shall understand the nature of socialist realism. Literature lessons shall enable and stimulate the pupils to read and appreciate works of literature by themselves.

— In addition to Russian a second foreign language is taught at the secondary stage; this is generally English.
The pupils shall be enabled to make themselves understood in the foreign languages and to read and understand simple texts of general or popular science content. Instruction in foreign languages shall promote the understanding of other nations.

— In the art subjects the pupils' conscious and practical artistic activities shall be promoted. Their ability to appreciate works of art shall be further enhanced, their aesthetic judgment developed, and their intellectual education promoted. The pupils shall be brought to feel a need to play an active part in cultural life.

—Physical training seeks specifically to increase, by an all-around basic physical training, the personal need of regular sports activities. A high level of performance in sport shall be achieved. All pupils shall acquire the sports badge, and the most talented of them the Olympiad badge. School sports shall contribute to the preservation of health, to enjoyment of life, and to a healthy and hygienic way of living on the part of the pupils.

Article 17

(1) In keeping with the higher demands made on education, and in accordance with the need of our young people to spend their leisure time in a purposeful way, and with their desire for creative activities, a high-quality, "whole-day" school education shall be introduced at all schools for a continually increasing number of pupils. Instruction and extracurricular education shall be closely connected.

(2) "Whole-day" school education shall give the young people the opportunity to engage, according to their inclinations and interests, in mathematics, natural science, technoligy, social sciences, art, literature, sport, and tourism and to develop their abilities and talents. It supports the pupils in their endeavours to do socially useful work and to feel that the responsibilities they have are part of social responsibility as a whole, and contributes towards developing pleasure in work, diligence, persistence, creative zest, and a feeling for beauty. In this connection special importance must be attached to activities in "whole-day" groups and "whole-day" classes, to club work of different kinds, and to the participation in Olympiads and competitions.

(3) During their holidays the pupils shall strengthen their physique and health in the community of happy and self-reliant young people. Organized games and excursions serve this purpose.

(4) The socialist enterprises and scientific institutions are obliged to promote 'whole-day" school education and organized holiday pursuits, to win specialists for running the club work, and to put facilities for culture, sports, etc. at the disposal of the school children. The socialist enterprises and the scientific institutions and organizations shall entrust the clubs with socially useful and interesting work.

(5) The teachers and educators are responsible for the "whole-day" school education which forms an integral part of the integrated process of education at schools. They shall include the Free German Youth organization, the "Ernst Thaelmann" pioneer organization,

the German Gymnastics and Sports Association, and other organizations in this process. They utilize the social resources of the children's and youth organizations for developing the intellectual interests of the pupils and for organizing interesting activities among the pupils.

(6) "Whole-day" school education shall be built up step by step in accordance with the economic possibilities.

APPENDIX B

A Survey of Topics Included in the Curriculum
of the Compulsory Educational Program
in Literature, Mathematics, Physics,
Astronomy, Chemistry, Biology,
Geography, History,
and Civics

TABLE 1

Literature*

Grade	Topics Included in the Curriculum
5	Further development of reading skills; work with texts including fairy tales, anecdotes from *Till Eulenspiegel*, short stories and episodes from longer stories and books, and children's books including *Robinson Crusoe* by Defoe; discussions concerning theater pieces, films, radio and television programs; and poems.
6	Further development of reading skills; work with texts including mythology (the *Odyssey*, the *Nibelungenlied*, *Prometheus*), fables (Aesop, Luther, LaFontaine, Lessing), stories and episodes from stories, poems (Goethe, Fontane, Brecht's ballads, Moerike, Ruernberg, Becher); children's books; and discussions concerning theater pieces, films. radio and television programs.
7	Literary works including fables, anecdotes from the past and present (Hebel, Kleist, Weiskopf), stories about contemporaries, Keller's short story *Kleider machen Leute*, poems (Brecht, Hebel, Goethe, Schiller, Weinert, Becher, and Weerth); books for young people (Beseler, Pantelejew, and Hugo); discussions concerning theater pieces, films, radio and television programs.
8	Introduction to socialist literature; the national literary heritage including German literature to 1700, German classical literature, revolutionary-democratic and early socialist literature of the nineteenth century, the literature of bourgeois realism after 1848; Russian and French literature of the nineteenth century; socialist literature (Brecht, Seghers, Sluckis, and Fuehmann); and discussions concerning the theater and theater attendance, films, radio and television productions.
9	The literature of bourgeois realism in its struggle against imperialism and war (H. Mann, A. Zweig, and Tucholsky); the contribution of Soviet literature in the construction of socialist society; the significance of German socialist literature in the struggle against imperialism and fascism; socialist literature of the German Democratic Republic (Apitz, Gotsche); poetry of the rising bourgeoisie (Lessing, Shakespeare's *Macbeth*, *Sturm und Drang*, and Goethe); films, theater, radio and television productions discussions and guidance.
10	German classical literature (Schiller, Part One of Goethe's *Faust*, selections from Heine's *Deutschland, Ein Wintermaerchen*); writers from the capitalist countries supportive of peace and humanism; socialist humanism in Soviet literature; the development of socialist national literature in the GDR.

* Neuner, pp. 326-29.

TABLE 2

Mathematics*

Grade	Topics Included in the Curriculum
1	Addition and subtraction of numbers up to 10 with sums no higher than 20; multiplication and division of numbers up to 20.
2	Addition and subtraction of numbers up to 100; multiplication and division of numbers up to 100; introduction to geometry including points, lines, angles, triangles, rectangles, and circles.
3	Addition, subtraction, multiplication, and division of numbers up to 10,000; geometry and geometrical drawing.
4	Series of natural numbers up to 1,000,000 including their graphical illustration and the concept of rounding-off numbers; basic operations with natural numbers; fundamental geometrical concepts.
5	Measurement and units of measure (linear and angular); addition and subtraction of fractions and decimals; fundamental geometrical concepts and construction.
6	Addition, subtraction, multiplication, and division of fractions; equations and proportionalities; plane geometry.
7	The slide rule and its use; addition, subtraction, multiplication, and division of rational numbers; solving equations and inequalities; square numbers and square roots; descriptive geometry including the concept of projection; circular measurement; solid geometry.
8	Calculations with variables; similarities; linear functions; area and volume calculations.
9	Real numbers and work with variables; systems of equalities and inequalities including linear inequalities and systems of two linear equations; potential and the potential function; quadratic functions and quadratic equations; exponential and logarithmic functions and the use of mathematical tables.
10	Trigonometry; solid geometry and the illustration of solids.

* Neuner, 153-58.

TABLE 3

Physics[*]

Grade	Topics Included in the Curriculum
6	Introduction to physics; bodies and matter (properties of physical bodies, volume, the motion of solid bodies, force and its effect on bodies, mass, the density of matter, the particle structure of matter, behavior of the volume of bodies when heated and cooled, temperature, change of state, thermal diffusion in matter, the structure of atoms and electric charge); optics (light sources and the propagation of light, reflection, refraction, and optical instruments.
7	Mechanics (force and its graphical illustration, mechanical work, simple machines, potential and kinetic energy, the law of conservation of energy, power); mechanics of liquids and gases (pressure of liquids and gases in a closed container, gravitational pressure and its effects, pressure relationahips in flowing liquids and gases).
8	Thermodynamics (heat energy including review and new material, equation of state for an ideal gas, transformation of energy and the first law of thermodynamics); electrical theory (charge, intensity, and electric potential); electrical energy, work, and power; electrical resistance, Ohm's law; unbranched and branched electrical current circuits.
9	Mechanics (foundations of kinematics including the types of motion, acceleration of gravity, life and work of Galileo, projectile motion; foundation of dynamics including vector diagrams, Newton's law, Newton's life and work, law of inertia; energy and the relation between potential and kinetic energy, energy transformation; circular motion; gravitation); electrical theory (electric field theory; magnetic field theory; electromagnetic induction; processes of electrical conduction—a general model and applications).
10	Nuclear physics (atomic structure, elementary particles, atomic nuclei, the development and significance of atomic physics); oscillations (mechanical oscillations, electromagnetic oscillations—alternating current and—oscillating circuits); waves (mechanical waves, electromagnetic waves including light waves, Herzian waves, and X-rays).

[*] Neuner, pp. 187-89.

TABLE 4

Astronomy[*]

Grade	Topics Included in the Curriculum
10	Introduction to astronomy; the planetary system (the earth as a celestial body; the earth's moon; planetary motion and the struggle surrounding the heliocentric system; description and planetary physics; astronautics); astrophysics and stellar astronomy (the sun, the stars, the Milky Way system and extra-galactic systems); a systematized survey of astronomy from a historical perspective; and, an observational program.

[*] Neuner, pp. 214-15.

TABLE 5

Chemistry*

Grade	Topics Included in the Curriculum
7	Matter and change in matter (matter and its properties, physical process—chemical reaction, the science of chemistry—the chemical industry); oxygen and oxidation; introduction to chemical abbreviation (formula, valence, the law of conservation of mass, the chemical equation); introduction to chemical calculation; hydrogen, reduction, "redox" reactions.
8	Atom and ion (atomic structure, the development of knowledge concerning the atom, ionic formation); chemical bonding (atomic bond, ionic bonding, transition from ionic to atomic bonding, the metallic bond, chemical reaction on the basis of atomic structure and chemical bonding); acids; bases; salts; periodic system of the elements; elements in main group VII; carbon as an element of main group IV; chemical calculation (mass relationships in chemical reactions, volume relations in chemical reactions); hydrocarbons (introduction to organic chemistry, alkanes, alkenes, alkynes, benzene, comparative treatment of hydrocarbons, technical extraction of hydrocarbons from petroleum and natural gas).
9	Chemical reaction (review and new material, chemical equilibrium, foundations of catalysis); some organic compounds with one functional group in the molecule; some organic compounds with several functional groups in the molecule; plastics, elastics, and chemical fibers.
10	"Redox" reaction and oxidation number; nitrogen as an element of main group V; sulfur as an element of main group VI; the science of chemistry as a productive force (the development of the science of chemistry and the chemical industry, physical-chemical foundations and economic problems in chemical-technological procedures, the contribution of chemical production to the development of the GDR national economy).

* Neuner, pp. 197-99.

TABLE 6

Biology[*]

Grade	Topics Included in the Curriculum
5	Introduction to the theory of life; structure and development, environmental relationships and capabilities of the vertebrate body (fish, amphibians, reptiles, bird, mammals); development and structure of seed plants.
6	The structure and importance of seed plants (important plant families); structure, development, and environmenal relationships of invertebrates and the work of their organs (important animal families).
7	Introduction to microscopy and cell theory (historical development of the microscope, structure and use of the microscope, introduction to cell theory); single-celled life (single-celled animals, single-celled plants, bacteria); multicellular plants (algae, fungi, mosses pteridophytes; cells, tissues, organs, organisms (universal functions of cells in single-celled organisms and occurence of cell groups with specific functions in multi-cellular organisms).
8	Introduction to human anatomy, physiology, and hygiene; metabolism and energy transformation (introduction to metabolism, nourishment and digestion, blood and lymph, respiration, metabolism and energy transformation, elimination); the skin; locomotion and body posture (locomotion and support organs and their functions, hygiene of the support and locomotor system, injuries of the support and locomotor system—first aid); sense and nerve functions (introduction to the combined action of sense organs and the nervous system, sense functions, nerve functions, hygiene of the sensory organs and the nervous system); hormones; reproduction and development (the process of reproduction, structure and functions of the sex organs, embryological development, post-natal development with emphasis on youth).
9	Anatomy and physiology of plants; organisms in their environment (living space, environment of animals and plants; the ecological potency of organisms; socialization of organisms; utilization and conservation of nature in the GDR).
10	Genetics (introduction, structure and function of hereditary factors, distribution of hereditory factors, mutation and modification, human genetics); evolutionary theory (the theory of evolution, evolution of plants and animals, the history of evolution, the origin of life on earth, the evolutionary development of mankind); breeding plants and animals (introduction, breeding goals, methods of breeding).

*Neuner, pp. 206-08.

TABLE 7

Geography[*]

Grade	Topics Included in the Curriculum
5	Introduction to geography; the lowland regions in the GDR; the rise of mid-level mountains in the GDR.
6	Capitalist countries in Europe (the Federal Republic of Germany, Northern Europe, Western Europe, the Alps region, and Southern Europe); socialist countries in Europe; an overview of Europe.
7	The map of the earth and grids and time zones; the Soviet Union (introduction, survey of its physical geography, an overview of its economic geography); Asia (introduction, Central and East Asia, Southeast and Southern Asia, West Asia).
8	Africa (political situation, the physical geography of Africa, its economic geography); America (introduction, physical geography, the United States, the economic geography of Latin America); Australia and the Polar regions.
9	Physical geology (introduction; the atmosphere including its physical characteristics, weather, and climate; the hydrosphere including the circulation of water, measures for the utilization of water; the lithosphere; the geological history of Central Europe; features of the earth's surface).
10	The economic geography of the socialist community of nations (introduction, populations, mineral wealth and energy, agriculture); the economic geography of the GDR (introduction, population, mineral wealth, water, industry, agriculture, regions of the GDR); contemporary problems (the systematization of economic-geographical knowledge with respect to the continual intensification of cooperation among the socialist countries; the treatment of regions with respect to their physical and economic-geographic aspects).

* Neuner, pp. 276-79.

TABLE 8

History*

Grade	Topics Included in the Curriculum
5	The work and conditions of existence of human beings in primitive society; the decline of primitive society and development of the first class-society in the ancient Orient (ancient Babylonian despotism); the highpoint of slavery in antiquity in ancient Greece and in the Roman Empire; the cultural accomplishments of antiquity.
6	The downfall of Roman slave-holding society and the decline of the Western Roman Empire; the origin of feudalism in Western and Central Europe; feudalism in Byzantium and in the Arabian caliphate; the full development of feudalism in Western and Central Europe; the nature of feudalism; early revolution in Germany (the intensification of the contradictions of feudalism, humanism and the Renaissance, Reformation and the Peasant War).
7	Major geographic discoveries and the beginnings of West European colonialism; the development of capitalism in England (the origin of accumulation, the seizure of power by the bourgeoisie, the founding of the United States, the industrial revolution, the nature of capitalism); the contradictions between European countries in the sixteenth and seventeenth centuries (the Thirty Years War, the highpoint of absolutism in France and Russia); Germany from 1648 to 1789; the French Revolution and its international significance; Germany in the process of its bourgeois transformation from 1789 to 1890; the victory of capitalism production relations in the advanced countries and the first activities of the working class.
8	The beginning of the workers' movement (Marx and Engels, publication of *The Communist Manifesto*); the Revolution of 1848-49; the development of capitalism in the second third of the nineteenth century; the struggle for national unity of Germany (the evolution of the German workers' movement, the establishment of the German *Reich*); the Paris Commune and its lessons; the history of the development of Germany from 1871 to the turn of the century (the Reich and its economic development, the struggle of the working class against Prussian-German militarism and the bourgeoisie, the gradual development of monopoly capitalism); the beginnings of imperialism and the development of the international workers' movement; the aggressive politics of German imperialism and the struggle of the German workers' movement against reaction and the danger of war; the First World War; the historical position of imperialism.

TABLE 8 (continued)

Grade	Topics Included in the Curriculum
9	The Great Socialist October Revolution and its international effects; the November Revolution in Germany; international developments in the middle of the 1930's (the construction of socialism in the Soviet Union, reactionary internal and external politics of the imperialist powers); the history of the German people from 1919 to 1933 (particularly, the highpoint of the class struggle and the end of the Weimar Republic); the fascist dictatorship in Germany (the intensification of international tensions and the struggle of the international and German working class movement against fascism and the danger of war); the Second World War and its consequences.
10	The main features of international development from 1945 to 1949; the struggle for an antifascist-democratic order in Germany (the establishment of the GDR); major features of international development from 1949 to 1961 (the consolidation of socialism, the decline of imperialist colonialism, the increasing aggressiveness of imperialism and the development of West German imperialism); establishment of the foundations of socialism in the GDR, and the class struggle between socialism and imperialism in the process of consolidating the socialist world system; characteristic phenomena and tendencies of the debate between socialism and imperialism since the beginning of the 1960's.

* Neuner, pp. 249-52.

TABLE 9

Civics*

Grade	Topics Included in the Curriculum
7	The GDR—our Socialist Fatherland: introduction to the major problems of the epoch of worldwide transition from capitalism to socialism and the progress of socialism on German soil; the communists indicate the goal and direction for the reconstruction of Germany after 1945 and the democratic reconstruction of East Germany; the major accomplishments of the working class and all workers in industry, agriculture, and in social and cultural areas under the leadership of the Socialist Unity Party; an historical overview of the development of the GDR and the FRG (characteristic features of the imperialistic state of the FRG; attainment of a socialist order in the GDR in the class struggle, particularly against West German imperialism; the increasing integration of the GDR in the socialist community of nations; the objective process of the increasingly strong separation between the socialist GDR and the imperialist FRG); the treatment of contemporary political problems.
8	The socialist constitution of the GDR; the introduction to the constitution and its preamble; the political, socio-economic, scientific, and cultural foundations of our socialist society and the class character of our socialist state; the contents, the relation and significance of basic rights and responsibilities of citizens and their conscientious observation; the structure and system of state management in the GDR; the tasks of young people in the realization of the goals set at the Eighth Party Congress of the SED; treatment of current political problems.
9	The regularity of social development to socialism and its achievement in the class struggle of the working class in the future: contents and effectiveness of the laws of social development discovered by Marx and Engels in the present (Marxism-Leninism as the theoretical basis of the politics of Marxist-Leninist parties) and, the inhumane nature of capitalism and its decline and the objective basis of the historical mission of the working class; attainment of the destruction of imperialism and the victory of socialism, the realization of the historical mission of the working class in our epoch in the difficult class struggle of the working class under the leadership of Marxist-Leninist parties; Leninism—the Marxism of our epoch (the nature of socialism and socialism as a humanitarian alternative to inhumane imperialism); treatment of current political and ideological problems.

TABLE 9 (continued)

Grade	Topics Included in the Curriculum
10	The process of world revolution in the present and basic questions of the construction of a socialist society in the GDR: the process of world revolution in the present (the transition from capitalism to socialism and communism; socialism determines the process of world revolution; basic questions of the strategy and tactics of international communism and workers' parties; the politics of imperialism); basic questions concerning the economic development of the GDR (socialist production methods; the fundamental economic law of socialism and the major task put forth by the Eighth Party Congress; the intensification of socialism; economic planning and management; socialist economic integration); the social and political order of socialism (classes and class relations in socialist society; the leading role of the working class and its Marxist-Leninist party; the nature of socialist society); the main features of the socialist world view and morality (Marxism-Leninism—the world view of the working class; basic features of socialist morality); treatment of special current problems.

* Neuner, pp. 265-67.

INDEX

Academy of Pedagogical Sciences of the GDR, 41; research in programmed learning by, 85; development of teaching methodology by and role of, 87.

Administration and planning, for integrated socialist educational system, 39; centralized nature of, 39-42; advantages of centralized policy in, 131.

Astronomy, topics of instruction 162.

Biology, topics of instruction, 164.

Chemistry, topics of instruction, 163.

Civics, topics of instruction, 168-169.

Classroom laboratories, teaching of science courses in, 110. 111; schematic diagram of, 113.

Communism, difference between fascism and, 5; Marx's definition of, 29; definition adopted by twenty-second Congress of the Communist Party of the Soviet Union of, 35.

Communist epistemology, 23; role of "practice" in, 24-26, 114; variation of human ability in, 76-77; *Sachwissen* and *Methodenwissen*, 101.

Communist ideology (Marxism-Leninism), role in East German society, 1; role in learning process, 53.

Communist morality, responsibility of the schools in development of, 36.

Communist Party, concept developed by Lenin, 31; contemporary role of, 35-36, 42.

Communist world-view, 23

Copy theory of knowledge, 26.

Creativity, controlled nature in GDR of, 131.

Curricula, first publication in post-war period of, 11; in compulsory education, 73-76.

Day of Instruction in Socialist Production, 63-65, 111.

Democratic centralism, principle of, 31.

Democratization of the German Schools, Law on the, 11.

Dialectical centralism, principle of, 31.

Dialectical materialism, 19; as methodological foundation for science and scientific investigation in socialist society, 20; the dialectical process in, 21-23; role of "practice" in, 25-26; learning theory in, 23-26; interrelation between natural science and, 33, 52; philosophy and ideology, 36.

Dialectics, Laws of, 21-23, 32-34.

Economic planning, fundamental purpose in the GDR of, 3.

Education in pre-1933 Germany, 6; influence of Nazi ideology on, 7; FRG return to precepts of, 8.

Education in the GDR: ultimate goal of, 2, 50; component of economic planning, 2; relation between economic development and, 2-3; factors influencing origin, 5-6, 8-9; immediate post-war situation, 9-10; role of German Central Administration for Education (GCAE) in establishment of, 10; role of German

(Education, cont.) Communist Party (KPD) in reconstruction of, 10; legal sanction provided for system of, 11; elimination of major features of pre-war German education in, 11; first uniform curricula for, 11; SED orders Marxist-Leninist orientation of instruction in, 14, 15; influence of Soviet pedagogical literature in development of, 15; polytechnical education in and Soviet basis of, 15-16; Law on the Integrated Socialist Educational System and, 18; focus on development of Communist mentality in compulsory period of, 36; role of science learning, 52-55; responsibility for resolving antagonism between mental and physical labor, 56-57, 108, 123; role of polytechnical instruction in, 60; learning process in, 79; scholastic achievement in, 86-87; uniform approach towards, 108; importance of Western knowledge of, 128; emphasis on science and mathematics, 129-30; emphasis on fundamental learning, 129; creativity in, 131; comparison between education in the FRG and, 133-34.

Educational research, aims of, 41.

Engels, Friedrich (1820-1895); study of motion, 21; theory of historical materialism, 28-29; work on interrelation between dialectical naterialism and science, 32; first systematic statement on theory of polytechnical education by, 57.

Extended secondary school, 44, 46.

Frankiewicz, Heinz, Professor Dr., conversation with, 124-129.

Geography, topics of instruction, 165.

German Democratic Republic (GDR), 1; role of Socialist Unity Party (SED), 1; economic achievements, 2-3; immediate post-war situation, 9; founding of, 13; precarious existence until mid-1952 of, 13; first steps towards conversion to socialist state, 13-14; ideological tensions in, 14; Western efforts at subversion of, 15; efforts in educating youth, 134.

Gifted youth, specialized schools for, 44.

Handicapped youth, special schools for, 44.

Historical materialism, 19, 26-30.

History, topics of instruction, 166.

Individualized programmed learning, utilization in compulsory education of, 85-86.

Instructional methods, difference between use of in socialist education and in the West, 80; three basic types of, 80-83.

Instructional period, general requirements for, 80; observations of, 112-18.

Integrated Socialist Educational System, Act or Law on, 17,151-57; relation between economic development and compulsory education in, 3; revolutionary change from traditional German approach to education effected by, 18; statements concerning curricula, textbooks, and teaching aids in, 73-74; statements concerning teacher training in, 89.

Integrated socialist educational system, components of, 39; administration and planning for, 39.

EAST EUROPEAN MONOGRAPHS

41. *Boleslaw Limanowski (1835-1935): A Study in Socialism and Nationalism.* By Kazimiera Janina Cottam. 1978.
42. *The Lingering Shadow of Nazism: The Austrian Independent Party Movement Since 1945.* By Max E. Riedlsperger. 1978.
43. *The Catholic Church, Dissent and Nationality in Soviet Lithuania.* By V. Stanley Vardys. 1978.
44. *The Development of Parliamentary Government in Serbia.* By Alex N. Dragnich. 1978.
45. *Divide and Conquer: German Efforts to Conclude a Separate Peace, 1914-1918.* By L. L. Farrar, Jr. 1978.
46. *The Prague Slav Congress of 1848.* By Lawrence D. Orton. 1978.
47. *The Nobility and the Making of the Hussite Revolution.* By John M. Klassen. 1978.
48. *The Cultural Limits of Revolutionary Politics: Change and Continuity in socialist Czecholslovakia.*
48. *The Cultural Limits of Revolutionary Politics: Change and Continuity in Socialist Czecholslovakia.* By David W. Paul. 1979.
49. *On the Border of War and Peace: Polish Intelligence and Diplomacy in 1937-1939 and the Origins of the Ultra Secret.* By Richard A. Woytak. 1979.
50. *Bear and Foxes: The International Relations of the East European States 1965-1969.* By Ronald Haly Linden. 1979.
51. *Czechoslovakia: The Heritage of Ages Past.* Edited by Ivan Volgye and Hans Brisch. 1979.
52. *Prime Minister Gyula Andrássy's Influence on Habsburg Foreign Policy.* By János Decsy. 1979.
53. *Citizens for the Fatherland: Education, Educators, and Pedagogical Ideals in Eighteenth Century Russia.* By J. L. Black. 1979.
54. *A History of the "Proletariat": The Emergence of Marxism in the Kingdom of Poland, 1870-1887.* By Norman M. Naimark. 1979.
55. *The Slovak Autonomy Movement, 1935-1939: A Study in Unrelenting Nationalism.* By Dorothea H. El Mallakh. 1979.
56. *Diplomat in Exile: Francis Pulszky's Political Activities in England, 1848-1840.* By Thomas Kabdebo. 1979.
57. *The German Struggle Against the Yugoslav Guerrillas in World War II: German Counter-Insurgency in Yugoslavia, 1941-1943.* By Paul N. Hehn. 1979.
58. *The Emergence of the Romanian National State.* By Gerald J. Bobango. 1979.
59. *Stewards of the Land: The American Farm School and Modern Greece.* By Brenda L. Marder. 1979.
60. *Roman Dmowski: Party, Tactics, Ideology, 1895-1907.* By Alvin M. Fountain II. 1980.
61. *International and Domestic Politics in Greece During the Crimean War.* By Jon V. Kofas. 1980.
62. *Fires on the Mountain: The Macedonian Revolutionary Movement and the Kidnapping of Ellen Stone.* By Laura Beth Sherman. 1980.
63. *The Modernization of Agriculture: Rural Transformation in Hungary, 1848-1975.* Edited by Joseph Held. 1980.
64. *Britain and the War for Yugoslavia, 1940-1943.* By Mark C. Wheeler. 1980.
65. *The Turn to the Right: The Ideological Origins and Development of Ukrainian Nationalism, 1919-1929.* By Alexander J. Motyl. 1980.

66. *The Maple Leaf and the White Eagle: Canadian-Polish Relations, 1918-1978.* By Aloysius Balawyder, 1980.
67. *Antecedents of Revolution: Alexander I and the Polish Congress Kingdom, 1815-1825.* By Frank W. Thackeray. 1980.
68. *Blood Libel at Tiszaeszlar.* By Andrew Handler. 1980.
69. *Democratic Centralism in Romania: A Study of Local Communist Politics.* By Daniel N. Nelson. 1980.